Credits

Author:
Ruth Maran

Copy Editors:
Raquel Scott
Roxanne Van Damme

Technical Consultant:
Paul Whitehead

Project Manager:
Judy Maran

Editors:
Teri Lynn Pinsent
Norm Schumacher
Megan Kirby

Screen Captures:
Jill Maran

Layout Artist:
Treena Lees

Illustrators:
Russ Marini
Steven Schaerer
Suzana G. Miokovic

Screen Artist and Illustrator:
Darryl Grossi

Indexer:
Teri Lynn Pinsent

Permissions Coordinator:
Jennifer Amaral

**Senior Vice President
and Publisher, Hungry Minds
Technology Publishing Group:**
Richard Swadley

**Publishing Director,
Hungry Minds Technology
Publishing Group:**
Barry Pruett

**Editorial Support,
Hungry Minds Technology
Publishing Group:**
Jennifer Dorsey
Sandy Rodrigues
Lindsay Sandman

Post Production:
Robert Maran

Acknowledgments

Thanks to the dedicated staff of maranGraphics, including
Jennifer Amaral, Roderick Anatalio, Darryl Grossi,
Kelleigh Johnson, Megan Kirby, Wanda Lawrie,
Treena Lees, Cathy Lo, Jill Maran, Judy Maran, Robert Maran,
Ruth Maran, Russ Marini, Suzana G. Miokovic, Stacey Morrison,
Teri Lynn Pinsent, Steven Schaerer, Norm Schumacher,
Raquel Scott, Roxanne Van Damme and Paul Whitehead.

Finally, to Richard Maran who originated the easy-to-use
graphic format of this guide. Thank you for your
inspiration and guidance.

Table of Contents

CHAPTER 1

WINDOWS BASICS

CHAPTER 2

VIEW FILES

CHAPTER 3

WORK WITH FILES

CHAPTER 4

WORK WITH MUSIC AND VIDEOS

CHAPTER 5

CREATE MOVIES

CHAPTER 6

SHARE YOUR COMPUTER

Table of Contents

CHAPTER 10

EXCHANGE E-MAIL

CHAPTER 11

EXCHANGE INSTANT MESSAGES

INTRODUCTION TO WINDOWS

Microsoft® Windows® XP is a program that controls the overall activity of your computer.

Microsoft Windows XP ensures that all parts of your computer work together smoothly and efficiently. **XP** stands for ex**p**erience.

Work with Files

Windows provides ways to manage the files stored on your computer. You can sort, open, rename, print, delete, move and search for files. You can also e-mail a file, publish a file to the Web and copy files to a floppy disk or recordable CD.

Customize Windows

You can customize Windows to suit your preferences. You can add a colorful picture to your screen, have sound effects play when certain computer events occur and adjust the volume of sound on your computer. Windows also allows you to set up a screen saver to appear when you do not use your computer for a period of time.

Work with Multimedia

Windows allows you to play music CDs and listen to radio stations that broadcast on the Internet. Windows also helps you find the latest music and movies on the Internet, organize your media files and copy songs from your computer to a recordable CD. You can also transfer your home movies to your computer so you can organize and edit the movies before sharing them with friends and family.

Share Your Computer

If you share your computer with other people, you can create user accounts to keep the personal files and settings for each person separate. You can assign a password to each user account and easily share files with other users.

Optimize Computer Performance

Windows provides tools to help you optimize your computer's performance. You can install new programs, update Windows and restore your computer to an earlier time if you experience problems. You can also allow a friend or colleague at another computer to view your computer screen and take control of your computer to help you solve a computer problem.

Work on a Network

Windows allows you to share information and equipment with other people on a network. You can share folders stored on your computer as well as a printer that is directly connected to your computer. Windows also provides a wizard to help you set up a network.

Access the Internet

Windows allows you to browse through the information on the World Wide Web. You can search for Web pages of interest and create a list of your favorite Web pages so you can quickly access the pages in the future. Windows also allows you to exchange electronic mail with people around the world. You can read, send, reply to, forward, print and delete e-mail messages. Windows also includes the Windows Messenger program that allows you to exchange instant messages and files over the Internet with friends and family.

You can use the Start menu to access programs, files, computer settings and help with Windows.

The programs available on the Start menu depend on the software installed on your computer.

USING THE START MENU

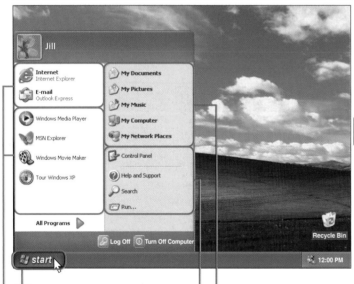

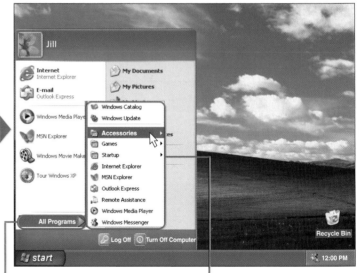

1 Click **start** to display the Start menu.

■ These items start your Web browser and e-mail program.

■ These items allow you to quickly start the programs you have most recently used.

■ These items allow you to quickly access commonly used locations.

■ These items allow you to change your computer's settings, get help, search for information and run programs.

■ If the Start menu displays the item you want to use, click the item.

2 If the item you want to use is not displayed on the Start menu, click **All Programs**.

■ A list of the programs on your computer appears. A menu item with an arrow (▶) will display another menu.

3 To display another menu, position the mouse ▷ over the menu item with an arrow (▶).

Which programs does Windows provide?

Windows comes with many useful programs.
Here are some examples.

Windows Media Player is a
program that allows you to find
and play media files, play music
CDs and listen to radio stations
that broadcast on the Internet.

Windows Messenger is a
program you can use to
exchange instant messages
and files with friends and
family.

Windows Movie Maker is a program
that allows you to transfer your
home movies to your computer
where you can then organize and
edit the movies.

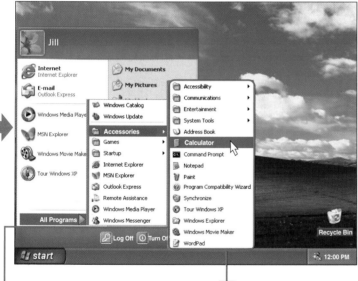

■ Another menu appears.

4 You can repeat step 3
until the item you want to
use appears.

5 Click the item you
want to use.

*Note: To close the Start menu
without selecting an item, click
outside the menu area.*

■ In this example, the
Calculator window
appears.

■ A button for the
open window appears
on the taskbar.

6 When you finish
working with the
window, click ✕ to
close the window.

You can use a scroll bar to browse through the information in a window. Scrolling is useful when a window is not large enough to display all the information it contains.

SCROLL THROUGH A WINDOW

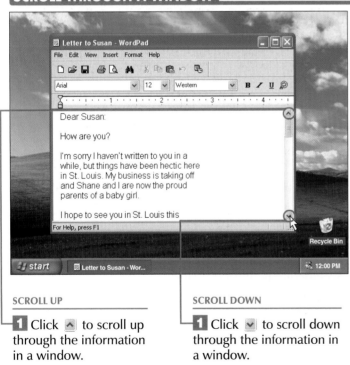

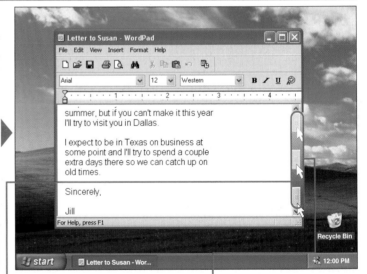

SCROLL UP

1 Click ▲ to scroll up through the information in a window.

SCROLL DOWN

1 Click ▼ to scroll down through the information in a window.

SCROLL TO ANY POSITION

1 Position the mouse over the scroll box.

2 Drag the scroll box along the scroll bar until the information you want to view appears.

■ The location of the scroll box indicates which part of the window you are viewing. For example, when the scroll box is halfway down the scroll bar, you are viewing information from the middle of the window.

CLOSE A WINDOW

When you finish working with a window, you can close the window to remove it from your screen.

CLOSE A WINDOW

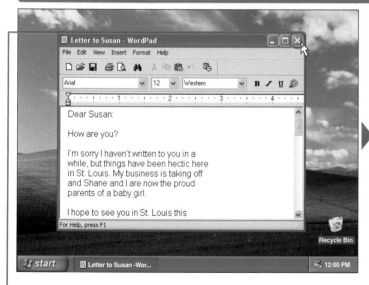

1 Click ☒ in the window you want to close.

■ The window disappears from your screen.

■ The button for the window disappears from the taskbar.

If a window covers items on your screen, you can move the window to a different location.

You may want to move several windows to see the contents of multiple windows at once.

MOVE A WINDOW

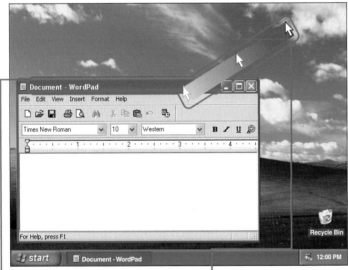

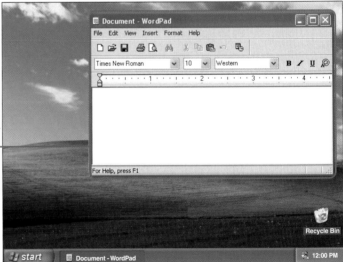

1 Position the mouse over the title bar of the window you want to move.

2 Drag the mouse to where you want to place the window.

■ The window moves to the new location.

Note: You cannot move a maximized window. For information on maximizing a window, see page 10.

8

RESIZE A WINDOW

You can easily change the size of a window displayed on your screen.

Enlarging the size of a window allows you to view more information in the window. Reducing the size of a window allows you to view items covered by the window.

RESIZE A WINDOW

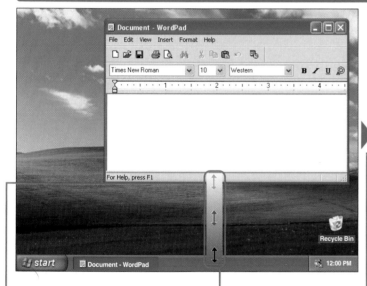

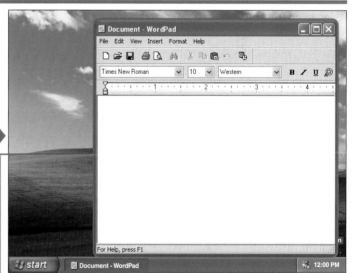

1 Position the mouse ↕ over an edge of the window you want to resize (↕ changes to ↕, ↔, ↗ or ↘).

2 Drag the mouse ↕ until the window displays the size you want.

■ The window displays the new size.

Note: You cannot resize a maximized window. For information on maximizing a window, see page 10.

MAXIMIZE A WINDOW

You can maximize a window to fill your entire screen. This allows you to view more of the window's contents.

MAXIMIZE A WINDOW

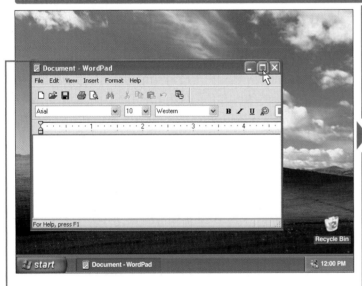

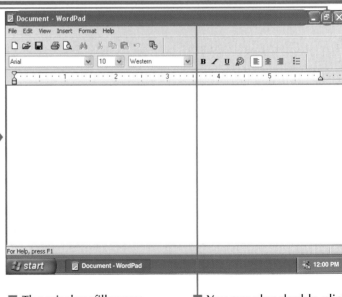

1 Click ⬜ in the window you want to maximize.

■ The window fills your entire screen.

■ To return the window to its previous size, click ⧉.

■ You can also double-click the title bar of a window to maximize the window.

10

MINIMIZE A WINDOW

If you are not using a window, you can minimize the window to temporarily remove it from your screen. You can redisplay the window at any time.

Minimizing a window allows you to temporarily put a window aside so you can work on other tasks.

MINIMIZE A WINDOW

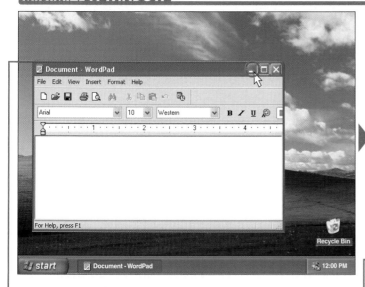

1 Click ■ in the window you want to minimize.

■ The window reduces to a button on the taskbar.

■ To redisplay the window, click its button on the taskbar.

Note: If a menu appears, displaying the names of several open windows when you click a button on the taskbar, click the name of the window you want to redisplay.

11

> If you have more than one window open on your screen, you can easily switch between the windows.

Each window is like a separate piece of paper. Switching between windows is like placing a different piece of paper at the top of the pile.

You can work in only one window at a time. The active window appears in front of all other windows and displays a dark title bar.

SWITCH BETWEEN WINDOWS

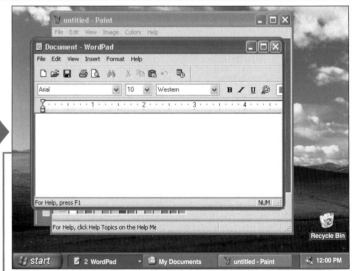

■ The taskbar displays a button for each open window. If you have many windows open, all the buttons for a program may appear as a single button on the taskbar.

1 To display the window you want to work with, click its button on the taskbar.

■ A menu may appear, displaying the name of each open window in the program.

2 Click the name of the window you want to display.

■ The window appears in front of all other windows. You can now clearly view the contents of the window.

Note: You can also click anywhere inside a window to display the window in front of all other windows.

12

CLOSE A MISBEHAVING PROGRAM

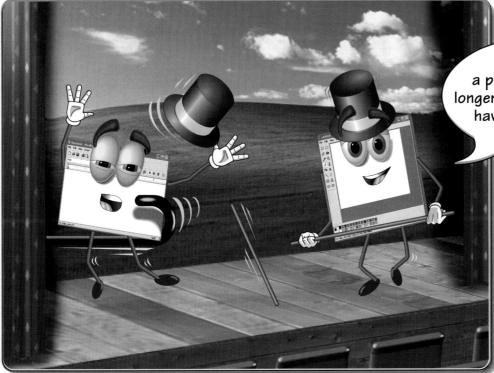

You can close a program that is no longer responding without having to shut down Windows.

When you close a misbehaving program, you will lose any information you did not save in the program.

Closing a misbehaving program should not affect other open programs.

CLOSE A MISBEHAVING PROGRAM

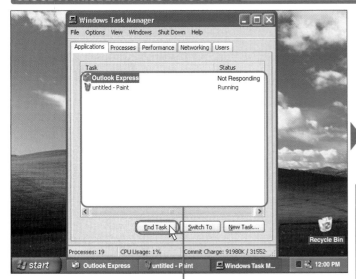

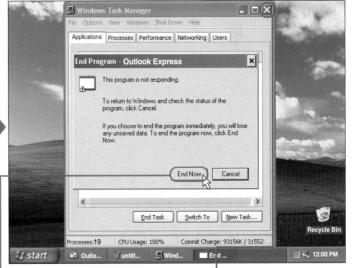

1 To close a misbehaving program, press and hold down the `Ctrl` and `Alt` keys as you press the `Delete` key.

■ The Windows Task Manager window appears.

■ This area lists the programs that are currently running. The phrase **Not Responding** appears beside the name of a misbehaving program.

2 Click the program that is misbehaving.

3 Click **End Task**.

■ The End Program dialog box appears, stating that the program is not responding.

4 Click **End Now** to close the program.

5 Click ☒ to close the Windows Task Manager window.

13

Windows includes several games that you can play on your computer. Games are a fun way to improve your mouse skills and hand-eye coordination.

You can play some games, such as Checkers, with other people on the Internet. Windows will match you with players from around the world. To play a game on the Internet, you will need an Internet connection.

PLAY GAMES

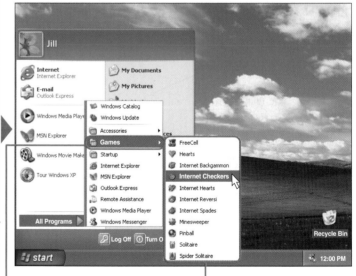

1 Click **start** to display the Start menu.

2 Click **All Programs** to view a list of the programs on your computer.

3 Click **Games**.

4 Click the game you want to play.

What games are included with Windows?

Here are some popular games included with Windows.

Minesweeper

Minesweeper is a strategy game in which you try to avoid being blown up by mines.

Pinball

Pinball is similar to a pinball game you would find at an arcade. You launch a ball and then try to score as many points as possible.

Solitaire

Solitaire is a classic card game that you play on your own. The object of the game is to place all the cards in order from ace to king in four stacks—one stack for each suit.

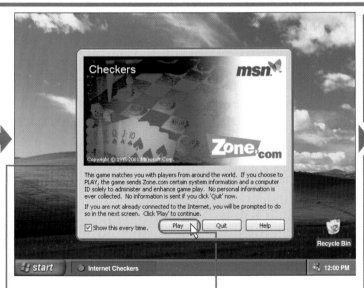 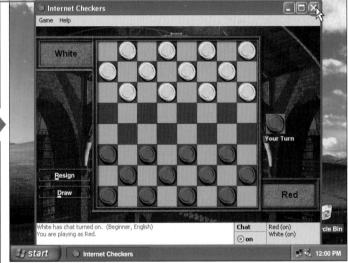

■ If you selected an Internet game, a dialog box appears that displays information about playing games on the Internet.

Note: If you selected a non-Internet game, skip to step 6.

5 Click **Play** to continue.

Note: If you are not currently connected to the Internet, a dialog box will appear that allows you to connect.

■ A window appears, displaying the game. In this example, the Internet Checkers window appears.

6 When you finish playing the game, click ⊠ to close the window.

■ A message may appear, confirming that you want to leave the game. Click **Yes** to leave the game.

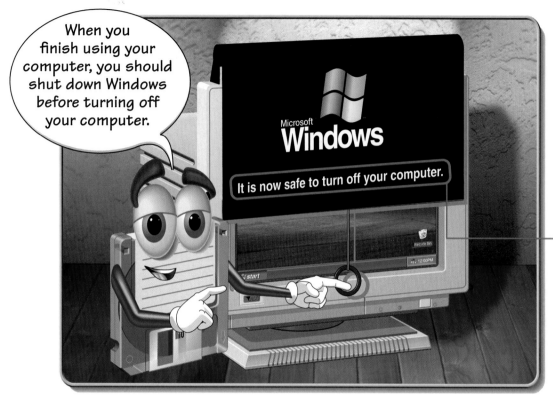

When you finish using your computer, you should shut down Windows before turning off your computer.

It is now safe to turn off your computer.

■ Do not turn off your computer until this message appears on your screen. Many computers will not display this message and will turn off automatically.

Before shutting down Windows, make sure you close all the programs you have open.

SHUT DOWN WINDOWS

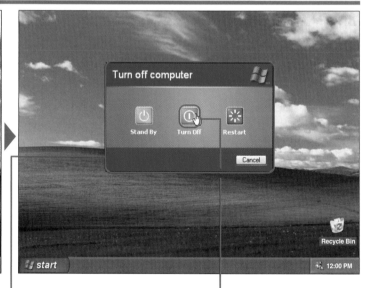

1 Click **start** to display the Start menu.

2 Click **Turn Off Computer**.

■ The Turn off computer dialog box appears.

3 Click **Turn Off** to shut down Windows.

RESTART YOUR COMPUTER

If your computer is not operating properly, you can restart your computer to try to fix the problem.

Before restarting your computer, make sure you close all the programs you have open.

RESTART YOUR COMPUTER

1 Click **start** to display the Start menu.

2 Click **Turn Off Computer**.

■ The Turn off computer dialog box appears.

3 Click **Restart** to restart your computer.

If you do not know how to perform a task in Windows, you can use the Help feature to find information on the task.

FIND HELP INFORMATION

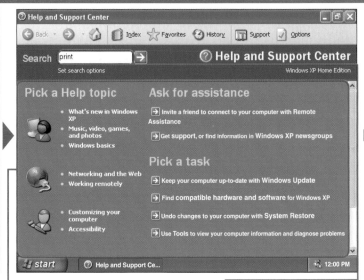

1 Click **start** to display the Start menu.

2 Click **Help and Support**.

■ The Help and Support Center window appears.

■ This area displays a list of common help topics, ways that you can ask for assistance and tasks for which you can receive help. You can click an item of interest to display information about the item.

3 To search for specific help information, click this area and then type a word or phrase that describes the topic of interest.

4 Press the **Enter** key to start the search.

Why do some help topics display colored text?

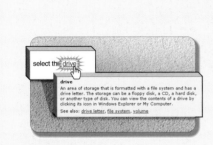

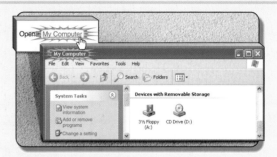

Display a Definition

You can click a word or phrase that appears in green to display a definition of the word or phrase. To hide the definition, click the definition.

Obtain Additional Help

You can click a word or phrase that appears in blue to obtain additional help. Windows may display another help topic or open a window that allows you to perform a task. If you click the phrase "Related Topics" at the bottom of a help topic, a list of related help topics appears. You can click the help topic of interest in the list.

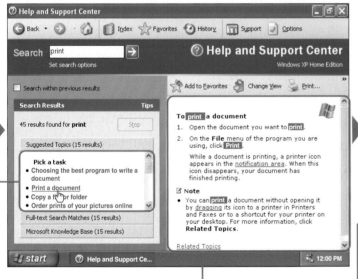

■ This area lists the help topics that match the information you entered.

5 Click a help topic of interest.

■ This area displays information about the help topic you selected. Windows highlights each occurrence of the word or phrase you searched for.

Note: You can repeat step 5 to display information for another help topic.

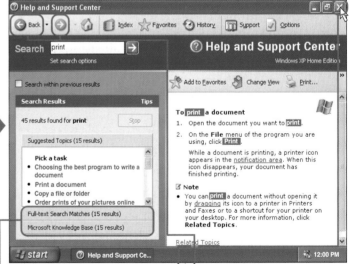

■ If you want to view a list of help topics under a different heading, click the heading of interest.

Note: To view a list of help topics under the Microsoft Knowledge Base heading, you must be connected to the Internet.

■ To browse through the help topics you have viewed, you can click **Back** or ➡.

6 When you finish reviewing help information, click ✕ to close the Help and Support Center window.

CHAPTER 2

VIEW FILES

Read this chapter to learn how to view the files and folders stored on your computer.

VIEW YOUR PERSONAL FOLDERS

Windows provides personal folders that offer a convenient place for you to store and manage your files. You can view the contents of your personal folders at any time.

Many programs automatically store files in your personal folders.

VIEW THE MY DOCUMENTS FOLDER

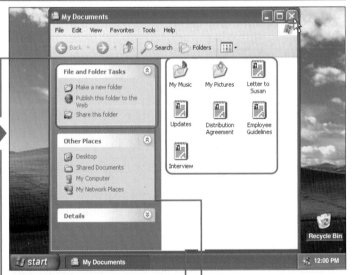

1 Click **start** to display the Start menu.

2 Click **My Documents** to view your documents.

■ A window appears, displaying the contents of the My Documents folder. This folder is useful for storing documents such as letters, reports and memos.

■ The My Documents folder contains the My Music and My Pictures folders.

■ This area displays options you can select to work with the documents in the folder.

3 When you finish viewing the contents of the My Documents folder, click ✕ to close the folder.

What tasks can I perform with the files in my personal folders?

The My Pictures and My Music folders offer several specialized options that you can select to work with your pictures and music. Here are some tasks you can perform.

MY PICTURES

View as a slide show

Displays all the pictures in the My Pictures folder as a full-screen slide show.

Order prints online

Sends the pictures you select to a Web site that allows you to order prints of the pictures.

MY MUSIC

Play all

Plays all the music in the My Music folder.

Shop for music online

Displays the WindowsMedia.com Web site, which allows you to listen to and purchase music.

VIEW THE MY PICTURES OR MY MUSIC FOLDER

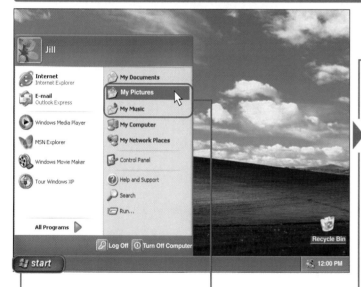

1 Click **start** to display the Start menu.

2 Click **My Pictures** or **My Music** to view your pictures or music.

■ A window appears, displaying the contents of the folder you selected.

■ In this example, the contents of the My Pictures folder appear. This folder displays a miniature version of each picture in the folder.

■ This area displays options you can select to work with the files in the folder.

3 When you finish viewing the contents of the folder, click ☒ to close the folder.

You can easily browse through the drives, folders and files on your computer.

Windows uses folders to organize the information stored on your computer.

VIEW CONTENTS OF YOUR COMPUTER

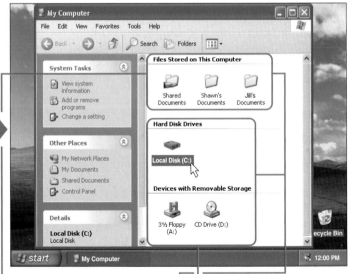

1 Click **start** to display the Start menu.

2 Click **My Computer** to view the contents of your computer.

■ The My Computer window appears.

Note: To view the contents of a floppy or CD-ROM drive, make sure you insert the floppy disk or CD-ROM disc into the appropriate drive before continuing.

■ The folders in this area contain files that all users set up on your computer can access. For more information on these folders, see pages 126 and 127.

■ The items in this area represent your hard drive, floppy drive, CD-ROM drive and any other drives available on your computer.

3 To display the contents of a drive or folder, double-click the item.

24

What do the icons in a window represent?

Each item in a window displays an icon to help you distinguish between the different types of items. Common types of items include:

	Folder
	Bitmap image
	Text document
	Windows Media Player file
	Document

How can I view information about a folder or file in a window?

To display information about a folder or file in a window, position the mouse over the folder or file. A yellow box appears, displaying information about the folder or file.

Type: Text Document
Date Modified: 7/13/2001 12:11PM
Size: 23.5 KB

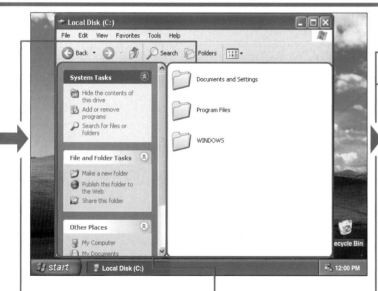

■ The contents of the drive or folder you selected appear.

*Note: If the contents of the drive you selected do not appear, click **Show the contents of this folder** in the window.*

■ This area displays options that you can select to perform common tasks and access commonly used locations on your computer. The available options depend on the selected item.

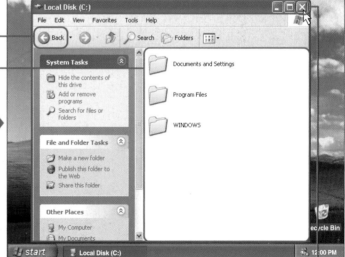

4 To continue browsing through the contents of your computer, you can double-click a folder to display its contents.

■ To return to a window you have previously viewed, click **Back**.

5 When you finish viewing the contents of your computer, click ☒ to close the window.

CHANGE VIEW OF ITEMS

You can change the view of items in a window. The view you select determines the way files and folders will appear in the window.

CHANGE VIEW OF ITEMS

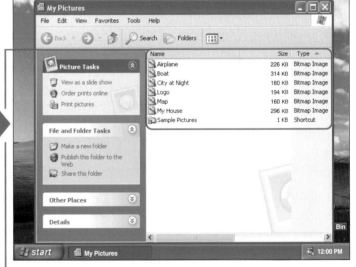

1 Click **View** to change the view of items in a window.

■ A bullet (●) appears beside the current view of the items.

2 Click the way you want to view the items.

■ In this example, the items appear in the Details view.

THE VIEWS

Filmstrip

The Filmstrip view displays pictures in a single row that you can scroll through. This view is only available in some windows, such as the My Pictures window. You can click a picture to display a larger version of the picture above the other pictures.

Thumbnails

The Thumbnails view displays a miniature version of each picture and some other types of files. If a miniature version of a file cannot be shown, an icon is displayed to indicate the type of file, such as a WordPad document (📄). In this view, miniature versions of a few pictures within a folder are shown on the folder's icon.

Tiles

The Tiles view displays items as large icons and displays information about each item below the item's file name. You can sort the items to change the information that each item displays. To sort items, see page 28.

Icons

The Icons view displays items as small icons with the file name appearing below each icon.

List

The List view displays items as small icons arranged in a list. This view is useful if you want to find a particular item in a long list of items.

Details

The Details view displays information about each item, including the name, size, type and date the items were last changed.

Name ▲	Size	Type	Date Modified
My Music		File Folder	7/6/2001 11:05 AM
My Pictures		File Folder	7/17/2001 8:27 AM
Projects		File Folder	7/17/2001 8:21 AM
Letter to Johnson	4 KB	Wordpad Document	7/13/2001 9:03 AM
Letter to Mary	5 KB	Wordpad Document	7/13/2001 9:04 AM
Memo	20 KB	Wordpad Document	7/13/2001 9:03 AM
Notes for Meeting	16 KB	Wordpad Document	7/6/2001 11:04 AM
Sales	8 KB	Wordpad Document	7/13/2001 9:03 AM

You can sort the items displayed in a window to help you find files and folders more quickly.

You can sort items by name, size, type or the date the items were last changed. Some windows allow you to sort items in other ways. For example, the My Music window allows you to sort items by artist, album title and track number.

SORT ITEMS

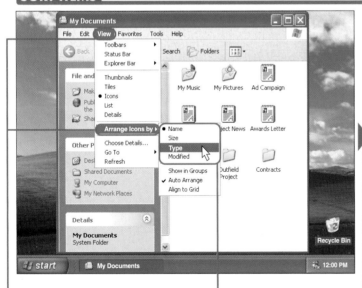

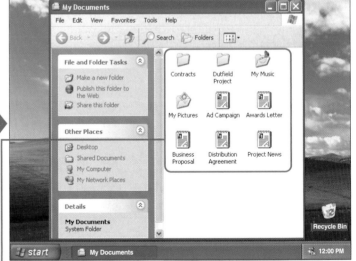

1 Click **View**.

2 Click **Arrange Icons by**.

3 Click the way you want to sort the items in the window.

■ The items appear in the new order. In this example, the items are sorted by type.

■ To sort the items in the reverse order, repeat steps **1** to **3**.

Note: You can only sort the items in the reverse order when viewing items in the List or Details view. To change the view of items, see page 26.

GROUP ITEMS

You can group items to better organize the files and folders in a window.

GROUP ITEMS

1 Click **View**.

2 Click **Arrange Icons by**.

3 Click **Show in Groups**.

Note: The Show in Groups option is not available when viewing items in the List or Filmstrip view. To change the view of items, see page 26.

■ Windows groups the items in the window.

■ You can sort the items to change the way the items are grouped in the window. For example, sorting the items by type will group the items by type. To sort items, see page 28.

■ If you no longer want to group the items in a window, repeat steps **1** to **3**.

29

Windows Explorer shows the organization of all the files and folders on your computer.

You can work with the files in Windows Explorer as you would work with files in any window. For example, you can move, rename and delete files in Windows Explorer. To work with files, see pages 34 to 73.

USING WINDOWS EXPLORER

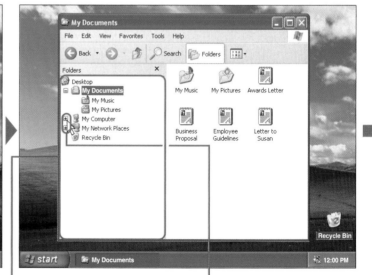

1 Click **start** to display the Start menu.

2 Click **All Programs** to view a list of the programs on your computer.

3 Click **Accessories**.

4 Click **Windows Explorer**.

■ A window appears.

■ This area displays the organization of the folders on your computer.

■ A folder displaying a plus sign (⊞) contains hidden folders.

5 To display the hidden folders within a folder, click the plus sign (⊞) beside the folder.

How can I quickly perform tasks with the files and folders displayed in Windows Explorer?

To quickly perform tasks in Windows Explorer, click the **Folders** button to display a list of options that you can select. The options that appear depend on the file or folder that is currently selected. To return to the organization of the folders, click the **Folders** button again.

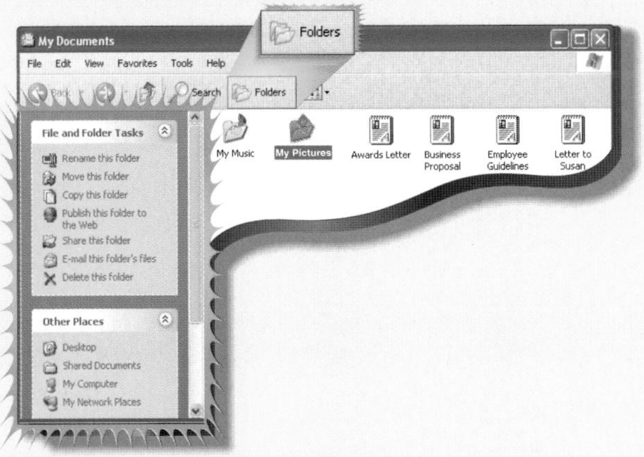

How can I view information about a file or folder displayed in Windows Explorer?

Position the mouse over a file or folder. After a few seconds, a yellow box appears, displaying information about the file or folder.

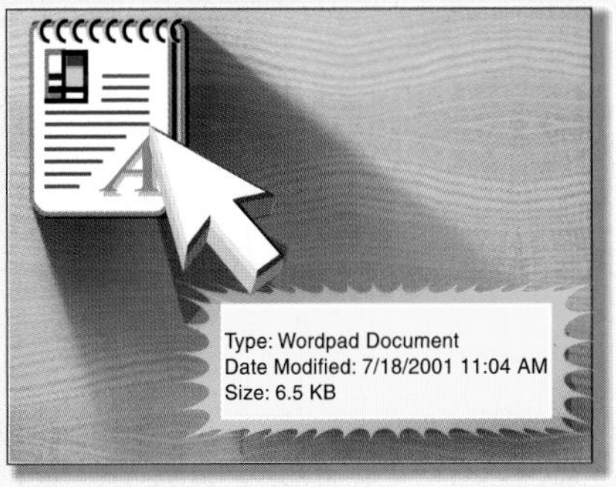

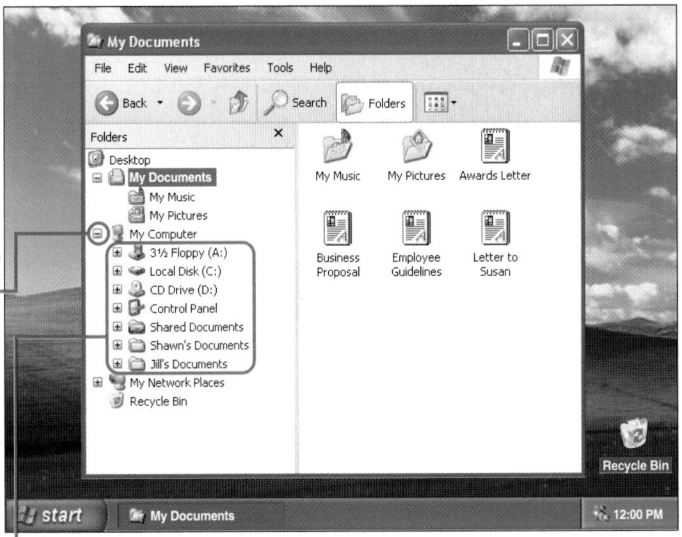

■ The hidden folders appear.

■ The plus sign (+) beside the folder changes to a minus sign (−). This indicates that all the folders within the folder are displayed.

Note: You can click the minus sign (−) to once again hide the folders within the folder.

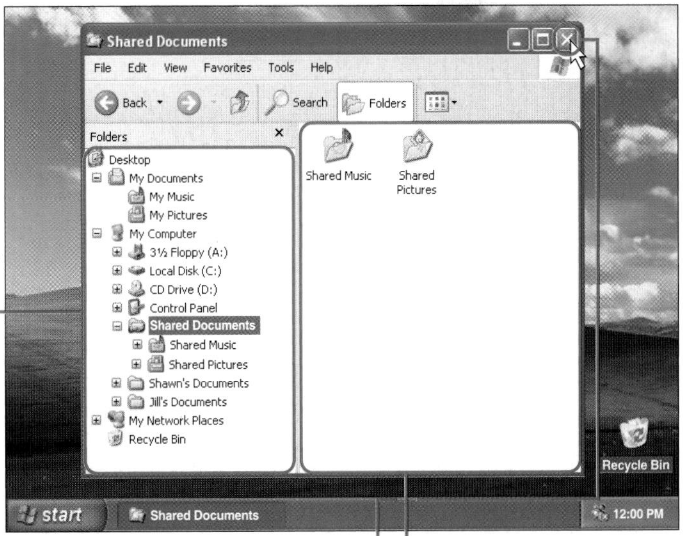

6 To display the contents of a folder, click the name of the folder.

■ This area displays the contents of the folder.

7 When you finish using Windows Explorer, click ☒ to close the window.

CHAPTER 3

WORK WITH FILES

This chapter teaches you how to manage your files efficiently. Learn how to print pictures, move and copy files, publish a file to the Web, copy files to a floppy disk or CD and much more.

SELECT FILES

Before working with files, you often need to select the files you want to work with. Selected files appear highlighted on your screen.

You can select folders the same way you select files. Selecting a folder will select all the files in the folder.

SELECT FILES

SELECT ONE FILE

1 Click the file you want to select. The file is highlighted.

2 If you want to display information about the file, click **Details**.

■ Information about the file appears, including the file type and the date and time the file was last changed.

*Note: To hide the information, click **Details** again.*

SELECT A GROUP OF FILES

1 Click the first file you want to select.

2 Press and hold down the **Shift** key as you click the last file you want to select.

How do I deselect files?

To deselect all the files in a window, click a blank area in the window.

To deselect one file from a group of selected files, press and hold down the **Ctrl** key as you click the file you want to deselect.

Note: You can deselect folders the same way you deselect files.

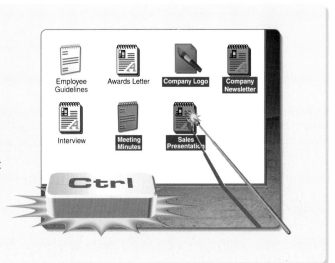

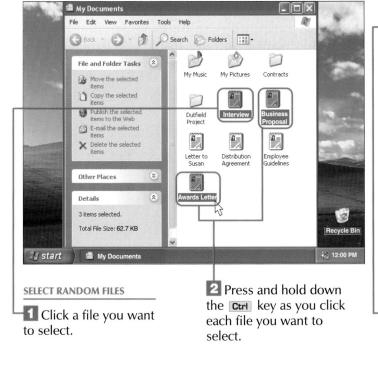

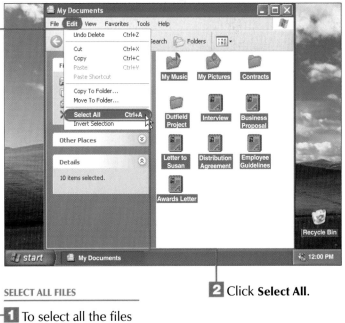

SELECT RANDOM FILES

1 Click a file you want to select.

2 Press and hold down the **Ctrl** key as you click each file you want to select.

SELECT ALL FILES

1 To select all the files and folders in a window, click **Edit**.

2 Click **Select All**.

You can open a file to display its contents on your screen. Opening a file allows you to review and make changes to the file.

You can open folders the same way you open files.

OPEN A FILE

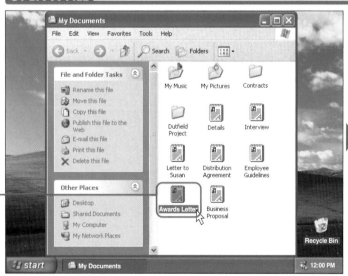

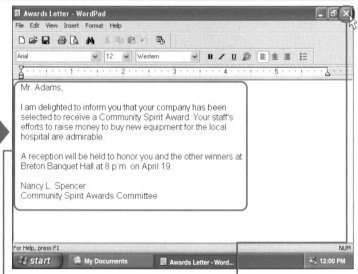

1 Double-click the file you want to open.

■ The file opens. You can review and make changes to the file.

Note: If you opened a picture, the picture appears in the Windows Picture and Fax Viewer window. To make changes to the picture, you will need to open the picture within the program you used to create the picture or in another image editing program.

2 When you finish working with the file, click ⊠ to close the file.

RENAME A FILE

You can rename a file to better describe the contents of the file. Renaming a file can help you more quickly locate the file in the future.

You can rename folders the same way you rename files. You should not rename folders that Windows or other programs require to operate.

RENAME A FILE

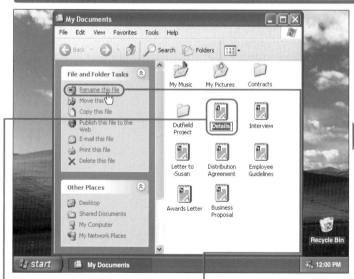

1 Click the name of the file you want to rename.

Note: You should not rename files that Windows or other programs require to operate.

2 Click **Rename this file** or press the F2 key.

■ A box appears around the file name.

3 Type a new name for the file and then press the Enter key.

*Note: A file name cannot contain the \ / : * ? " < > or | characters.*

■ If you change your mind while typing a new file name, you can press the Esc key to return to the original file name.

You can produce a paper copy of a file stored on your computer.

Before printing a file, make sure your printer is turned on and contains paper.

PRINT A FILE

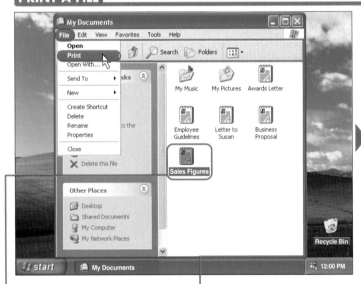

1 Click the file you want to print.

■ To print more than one file, select all the files you want to print. To select multiple files, see page 34.

2 Click **File**.

3 Click **Print**.

Note: If you selected a picture, the Photo Printing Wizard appears. For information on using the Photo Printing Wizard to print pictures, see page 40.

■ Windows quickly opens, prints and then closes the file.

■ When you print a file, a printer icon (🖶) appears in this area. The printer icon disappears when the file has finished printing.

How can I stop a file from printing?

You may want to stop a file from printing if you accidentally selected the wrong file or if you want to make last-minute changes to the file.

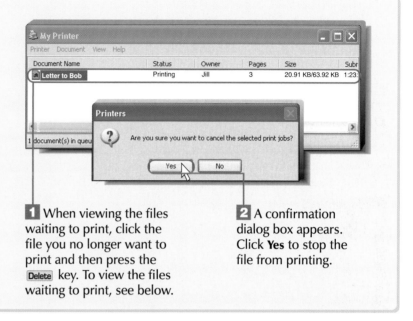

1 When viewing the files waiting to print, click the file you no longer want to print and then press the **Delete** key. To view the files waiting to print, see below.

2 A confirmation dialog box appears. Click **Yes** to stop the file from printing.

PRINT A FILE LOCATED ON THE DESKTOP

1 Right-click the file you want to print. A menu appears.

2 Click **Print** to print the file.

■ Windows quickly opens, prints and then closes the file.

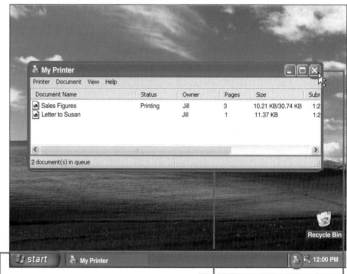

VIEW FILES WAITING TO PRINT

1 Double-click the printer icon (🖨) to view information about the files waiting to print.

Note: If the printer icon is not displayed, the files have finished printing.

■ A window appears, displaying information about each file waiting to print. The file at the top of the list will print first.

2 When you finish viewing the information, click ☒ to close the window.

39

Photo Printing Wizard

You can use the Photo Printing Wizard to print your pictures.

You can obtain pictures on the Internet, purchase pictures at computer stores or use a drawing program to create your own pictures. Windows also includes a few sample pictures.

PRINT PICTURES

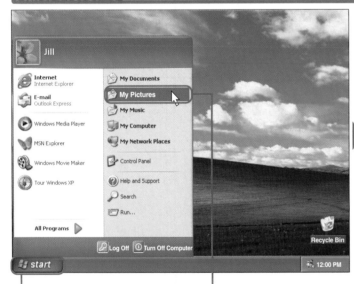

1 Click **start** to display the Start menu.

2 Click **My Pictures** to view the pictures stored in your My Pictures folder.

■ The contents of the My Pictures folder appear.

3 Click **Print pictures** to print the pictures in the folder.

Note: To print the pictures in a subfolder within the My Pictures folder, click the subfolder before performing step 3.

How can I get the best results when printing pictures?

Use High-Quality Paper
Your printer may allow you to use high-quality, glossy paper that is specifically designed for printing pictures. This type of paper will produce the best results when printing pictures.

Select a High Resolution
Make sure your printer is set to the highest possible resolution. A higher resolution will usually result in higher-quality pictures, but the pictures may take longer to print.

Can I use the Photo Printing Wizard to print pictures that are not stored in the My Pictures folder?

Yes. When you print a picture stored in another location on your computer, the Photo Printing Wizard will automatically appear to help you print the picture. You can print a picture stored in another location on your computer as you would print any file. For information on printing a file, see page 38.

■ The Photo Printing Wizard appears.

■ This area describes the wizard.

4 Click **Next** to continue.

■ This area displays a miniature version of each picture in the folder. Windows will print each picture that displays a check mark (✔).

5 To add (☑) or remove (☐) a check mark from a picture, click the check box (☐) for the picture.

■ To quickly select or deselect all the pictures, click **Select All** or **Clear All**.

6 Click **Next** to continue.

CONTINUED

PRINT PICTURES

The Photo Printing Wizard allows you to select the layout you want to use for the printed pictures.

Wallet Prints

5x7

8x10

3.5x5

You can select a layout that prints more than one picture on a page. Some layouts may crop part of a large picture so the picture will fit better on a page.

PRINT PICTURES (CONTINUED)

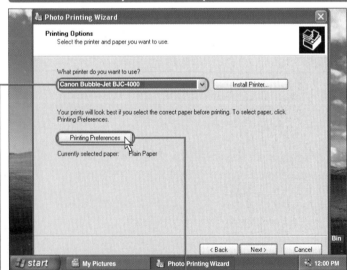

■ This area displays the printer you will use to print the pictures. You can click this area to select a different printer.

7 Click **Printing Preferences** to select the paper you want to use to print the pictures.

■ A Properties dialog box for the printer appears.

■ This area indicates where the paper you will use is located in the printer. You can click this area to change the paper source.

■ This area displays the type of paper you will use to print your pictures. You can click this area to change the type of paper.

Note: The available settings depend on your printer.

8 Click **OK** to confirm your changes.

9 Click **Next** to continue.

What other tasks can I perform with my pictures?

The My Pictures folder offers several options that you can select to perform tasks with your pictures.

View as a slide show

Displays all the pictures in the My Pictures folder as a full-screen slide show.

Order prints online

Sends the pictures you select to a Web site that allows you to order prints of the pictures.

Set as desktop background

Uses the picture you select as your desktop background. For information on changing the desktop background, see page 132.

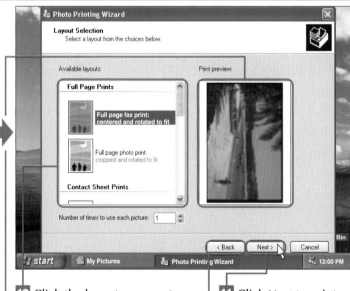

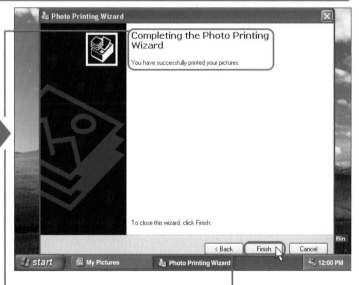

■10 Click the layout you want to use for your pictures.

■ This area displays a preview of how the pictures will appear on a printed page.

■11 Click **Next** to print the pictures.

■ You can click **Back** to return to a previous step and change your selections.

■ Windows prints the pictures.

■ This area indicates that you have successfully completed the Photo Printing Wizard.

■12 Click **Finish** to close the wizard.

You can delete a file you no longer need.

Before you delete a file, make sure you will no longer need the file. You should also make sure you do not delete a file that Windows or other programs require to operate.

DELETE A FILE

1 Click the file you want to delete.

■ To delete more than one file, select all the files you want to delete. To select multiple files, see page 34.

2 Click **Delete this file** or press the Delete key.

*Note: If you selected multiple files, click **Delete the selected items** in step 2.*

■ The Confirm File Delete dialog box appears.

3 Click **Yes** to delete the file.

How can I permanently delete a file
from my computer?

When you delete a file, Windows places
the file in the Recycle Bin in case you later
want to restore the file. If you do not want
to place a deleted file in the Recycle Bin,
such as when deleting a confidential file,
you can permanently delete the file from
your computer.

To permanently delete a file from your
computer, perform steps 1 to 3 on
page 44, except press and hold down
the Shift key as you perform step 2.

■ The file disappears.

■ Windows places the
file in the Recycle Bin in
case you later want to
restore the file.

*Note: To restore a file from the
Recycle Bin, see page 46.*

DELETE A FOLDER

**You can delete a folder and
all the files it contains.**

1 Click the folder you
want to delete.

2 Click **Delete this folder**
or press the Delete key.

■ The Confirm Folder
Delete dialog box appears.

3 Click **Yes** to delete the
folder.

RESTORE A DELETED FILE

The Recycle Bin stores all the files you have deleted. You can easily restore any file in the Recycle Bin to its original location on your computer.

You can restore folders the same way you restore files. When you restore a folder, Windows restores all the files in the folder.

RESTORE A DELETED FILE

■ The appearance of the Recycle Bin indicates whether or not the bin contains deleted files.

  Contains deleted files.

  Does not contain deleted files.

1 Double-click **Recycle Bin**.

■ The Recycle Bin window appears, displaying all the files you have deleted.

2 Click the file you want to restore.

■ To restore more than one file, select all the files you want to restore. To select multiple files, see page 34.

3 Click **Restore this item**.

*Note: If you selected multiple files, click **Restore the selected items** in step 3.*

Why is the file I want to restore not in the Recycle Bin?

The Recycle Bin does not store files you deleted from your network or from removable storage media such as a floppy disk. Files deleted from these locations are permanently deleted and cannot be restored. Files that are larger than the storage capacity of the Recycle Bin are also permanently deleted.

Can I permanently remove one file from the Recycle Bin?

You may want to permanently remove one file from the Recycle Bin, such as a file that contains confidential information. You can permanently remove a file from the Recycle Bin as you would delete any file on your computer. To delete a file, see page 44.

■ The file disappears from the Recycle Bin window and returns to its original location on your computer.

4 Click ⊠ to close the Recycle Bin window.

EMPTY THE RECYCLE BIN

You can empty the Recycle Bin to create more free space on your computer. When you empty the Recycle Bin, the files are permanently removed and cannot be restored.

1 Right-click **Recycle Bin**. A menu appears.

2 Click **Empty Recycle Bin**.

■ The Confirm Multiple File Delete dialog box appears.

3 Click **Yes** to permanently delete all the files in the Recycle Bin.

MOVE A FILE

You can move a file to a new location on your computer to re-organize your files.

When you move a file, the file will disappear from its original location and appear in the new location.

You can move a folder the same way you move a file. When you move a folder, all the files in the folder are also moved.

MOVE A FILE

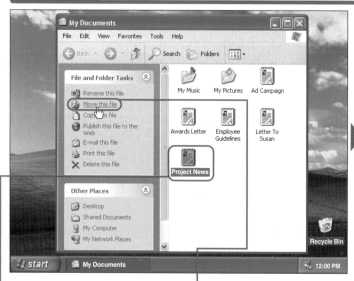

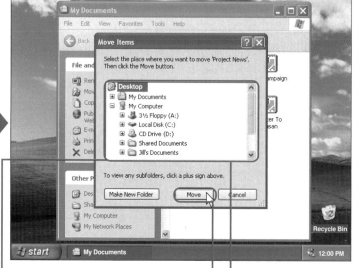

1 Click the file you want to move.

■ To move more than one file at once, select all the files you want to move. To select multiple files, see page 34.

2 Click **Move this file**.

*Note: If you selected multiple files, click **Move the selected items** in step 2.*

■ The Move Items dialog box appears.

■ This area displays the locations where you can move the file. A location displaying a plus sign (⊞) contains hidden items.

■ To display the hidden items within a location, click the plus sign (⊞) beside the location (⊞ changes to ⊟).

3 Click the location where you want to move the file.

4 Click **Move** to move the file.

48

Why would I want to move a file?

You may want to move a file to a different folder to keep files of the same type in one location on your computer. For example, you can move all your documents to the My Documents folder provided by Windows. Windows also includes the My Pictures and My Music folders that you can use to store your pictures and music files. To open one of these folders, see page 22.

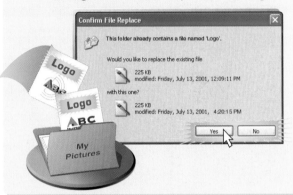

Why does a dialog box appear when I try to move a file?

If you try to move a file to a folder that contains a file with the same name, a dialog box appears, confirming the move. You can click **Yes** or **No** in the dialog box to specify if you want to replace the existing file with the file you are moving.

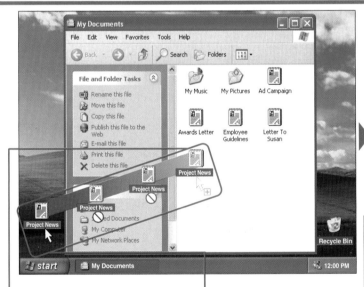

USING DRAG AND DROP

■ Before moving a file, make sure you can clearly see the location where you want to move the file.

1 Position the mouse ⟍ over the file you want to move.

■ To move more than one file at once, select all the files you want to move. Then position the mouse ⟍ over one of the files. To select multiple files, see page 34.

2 Drag the file to a new location.

■ The file moves to the new location.

■ The file disappears from its original location.

You can copy a file to a new location on your computer.

When you copy a file, the file appears in both the original and new locations.

You can copy a folder the same way you copy a file. When you copy a folder, all the files in the folder are also copied.

COPY A FILE

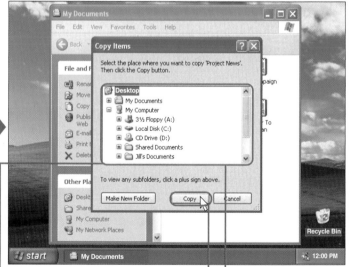

1 Click the file you want to copy.

■ To copy more than one file at once, select all the files you want to copy. To select multiple files, see page 34.

2 Click **Copy this file**.

*Note: If you selected multiple files, click **Copy the selected items** in step 2.*

■ The Copy Items dialog box appears.

■ This area displays the locations where you can copy the file. A location displaying a plus sign (☐) contains hidden items.

3 To display the hidden items within a location, click the plus sign (☐) beside the location (☐ changes to ☐).

4 Click the location where you want to copy the file.

5 Click **Copy** to copy the file.

Can I copy a file to the same folder that contains the file?

Yes. If you copy a file to the same folder that contains the file, Windows will add "Copy of" to the new file name. Copying a file to the same folder is useful if you plan to make major changes to a file, but you want to keep the original copy of the file. This gives you two copies of the file—the original file and a file that you can change.

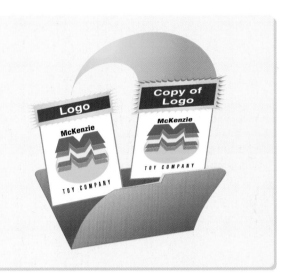

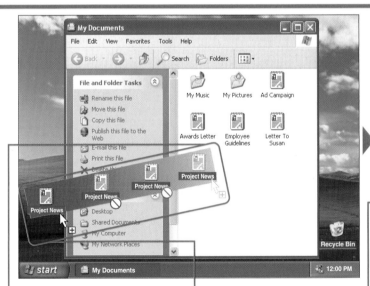

USING DRAG AND DROP

■ Before copying a file, make sure you can clearly see the location where you want to copy the file.

1 Position the mouse ⫽ over the file you want to copy.

■ To copy more than one file at once, select all the files you want to copy. Then position the mouse over one of the files. To select multiple files, see page 34.

2 Press and hold down the Ctrl key as you drag the file to a new location.

■ A copy of the file appears in the new location.

■ The original file remains in the original location.

You can e-mail a file to a friend, colleague or family member. You must have an e-mail account set up on your computer to be able to e-mail a file.

You can e-mail many types of files, including documents, pictures, videos and sounds. The computer receiving the file must have the necessary hardware and software installed to display or play the file.

E-MAIL A FILE

1 Click the file you want to send in an e-mail message.

■ To send more than one file in an e-mail message, select all the files you want to send. To select multiple files, see page 34.

2 Click **E-mail this file**.

*Note: If you selected multiple files, click **E-mail the selected items** in step 2.*

■ A window appears that allows you to compose a message.

3 Type the e-mail address of the person you want to receive the message.

Note: To send the message to more than one person, separate each e-mail address with a semicolon (;).

4 Windows uses the name of the file as the subject. To specify a different subject, drag the mouse I over the subject and then type a new subject.

Why does a dialog box appear when I try to e-mail a picture?

Windows can change the file size and dimensions of a picture you are sending in an e-mail message so the picture will transfer faster over the Internet and fit better on a recipient's computer screen. Reducing the file size of a picture is useful when you are e-mailing a large picture, since most companies that provide e-mail accounts do not allow you to send messages larger than 2 MB.

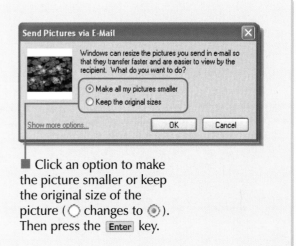

■ Click an option to make the picture smaller or keep the original size of the picture (○ changes to ◉). Then press the Enter key.

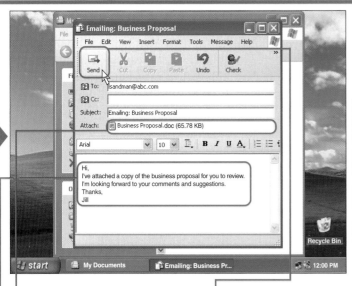

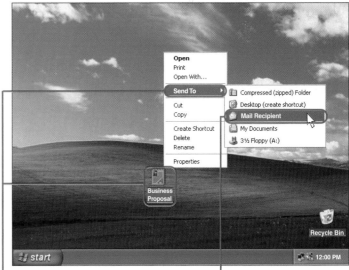

■ This area displays the name and size of the file you selected.

5 Windows includes a message that indicates that your files are attached. To use a different message, drag the mouse I over the message and then type a new message.

6 Click **Send** to send the message.

Note: If you are not currently connected to the Internet, a dialog box will appear that allows you to connect.

E-MAIL A FILE LOCATED ON THE DESKTOP

1 Right-click the file you want to send in an e-mail message. A menu appears.

2 Click **Send To**.

3 Click **Mail Recipient**.

4 Perform steps 3 to 6 starting on page 52 to compose and send the message.

PUBLISH A FILE TO THE WEB

You can publish files, such as documents and pictures, to the Web to allow friends, family and colleagues to view the files.

If you have just one or two small files that you want to share with another person, you may want to send the files in an e-mail message instead. To send files in an e-mail message, see page 210.

PUBLISH A FILE TO THE WEB

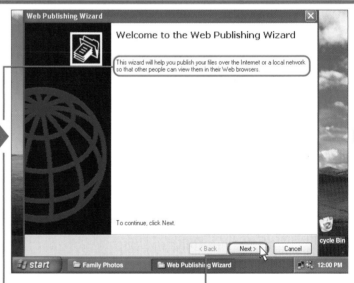

1 Click the file you want to publish to the Web.

■ To publish more than one file, select all the files you want to publish. To select multiple files, see page 34.

2 Click **Publish this file to the Web**.

*Note: If you selected multiple files, click **Publish the selected items to the Web** in step 2.*

■ The Web Publishing Wizard appears.

■ This area describes the wizard.

3 Click **Next** to continue.

Why does the Web Publishing Wizard ask me to set up an account after I choose a service provider?

The first time you publish a file to the Web, you will need to set up an account with a service provider. Follow the instructions on your screen to set up an account. When you set up an account, you may be required to obtain a Passport, which allows you to access many services on the Internet using a single user name and password. If you have previously set up an account, you may be asked to log in to your account to continue.

■ This area displays the contents of the folder that stores the file you selected to publish. Windows will publish each file that displays a check mark (✔).

4 To add (☑) or remove (☐) a check mark from a file, click the check box (☐) for the file.

5 Click **Next** to continue.

Note: If you are not currently connected to the Internet, a dialog box will appear, allowing you to connect.

6 Click the service provider you want to publish the file.

7 Click **Next** to continue.

Note: The following screens depend on the service provider you selected. A service provider may occasionally change the options displayed in the screens to make the wizard easier to use or to provide different options.

CONTINUED

55

If you selected the MSN service provider to publish your file, you can choose to share the file with other people or publish the file for your own private use.

PUBLISH A FILE TO THE WEB (CONTINUED)

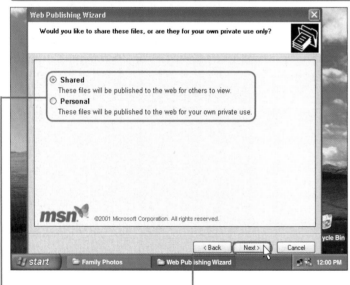

8 Click an option to specify if you want to publish the file for others to view or for your own private use (○ changes to ◉).

9 Click **Next** to continue.

Note: If you selected **Personal** *in step 8, skip to step 16.*

10 To create a community on the Web where you want to publish the file, click this option.

11 Click **Next** to continue.

Note: If you have previously created a community on the Web, click the name of the community in step 10 and then skip to step 16.

Why would I publish a file for my own private use?

You can publish a file for your own private use to store a backup copy of an important file in case your computer fails or you accidentally erase the file. You can also publish a file so you can access the file from many locations. For example, you can publish a presentation that you plan to deliver so you can access the presentation from any location.

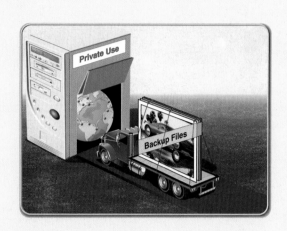

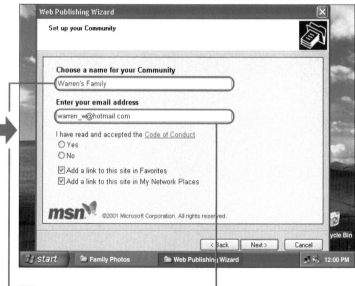

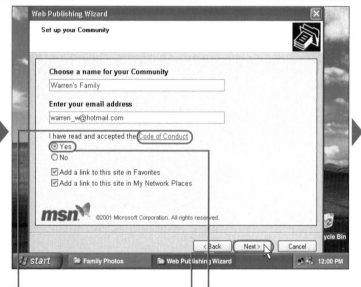

12 Type a name for the community you want to create to store the files you publish.

■ This area displays your e-mail address.

13 To display the code of conduct for MSN Web communities, click **Code of Conduct**.

■ When you finish reviewing the code of conduct, click ⊠ to close the MSN Code of Conduct window.

14 Click **Yes** to accept the code of conduct (○ changes to ◉).

15 Click **Next** to continue.

CONTINUED

If you are publishing a picture, the Web Publishing Wizard can adjust the size of the picture so it will transfer faster and be easier to view on a computer screen.

PUBLISH A FILE TO THE WEB (CONTINUED)

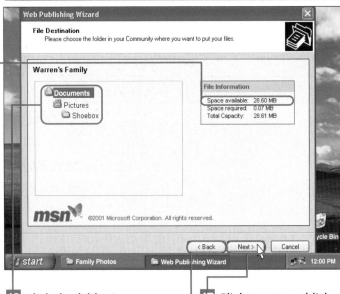

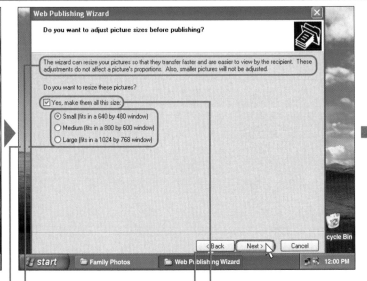

16 Click the folder in your community where you want to publish the file.

■ This area displays the amount of space available in your community.

17 Click **Next** to publish the file to the Web.

■ You can click **Back** to return to a previous step and change your selections.

■ If you are publishing a picture, the wizard can resize the picture.

Note: If this message does not appear, skip to step 20.

18 Click the size you want to use for the picture (○ changes to ◉).

■ If you do not want to resize the picture, click this option (☑ changes to ☐).

19 Click **Next** to publish the file to the Web.

How can I manage the files I published to the Web?

My Network Places

After you publish files to the Web, the My Network Places window may contain a folder that stores links to the files you have published. When you are connected to the Internet, you can add or delete files in the folder to add or delete the files on the Web. To open the My Network Places window, see page 170.

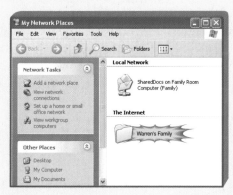

Web Page Favorites

Your list of favorite Web pages may also display a link to the Web site where you published the files. You can use this link to quickly display your published files. To view your list of favorite Web pages, see page 199.

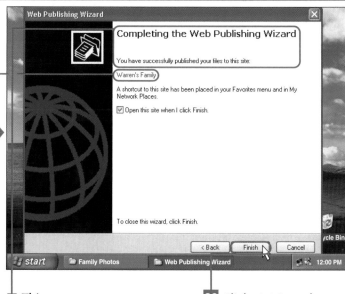

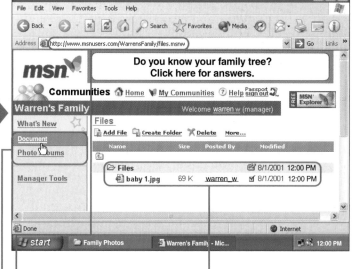

■ This message appears when you have successfully published the file to the Web.

■ This area displays the MSN Web community where the file can be accessed.

20 Click **Finish** to close the wizard.

■ The Microsoft Internet Explorer window appears, displaying the Web site where you published the file.

■ This area displays the Web page address where the file can be accessed.

21 Click the folder where you published the file.

■ The name of the file you published appears in this area. To view the file, click the name of the file.

Note: If you published the file to a photo album, you need to click the name of the album to view the file name.

CREATE A NEW FILE

You can instantly create, name and store a new file in the location you want without starting a program.

Creating a new file without starting a program allows you to focus on the organization of your files rather than the programs you need to accomplish your tasks.

CREATE A NEW FILE

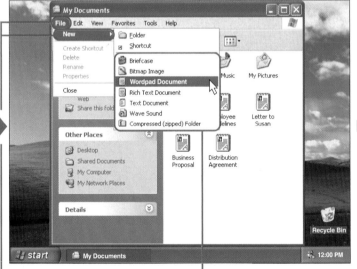

1 Display the contents of the folder you want to contain a new file.

Note: To browse through the folders on your computer, see pages 22 to 25.

2 Click **File**.

3 Click **New**.

4 Click the type of file you want to create.

SIMPLIFY IT

What types of files can I create?

The types of files you can create depend on the programs installed on your computer. By default, Windows allows you to create the following types of files.

File Type	Description
Briefcase	Stores copies of files that you want to work with on another computer.
Bitmap Image	Creates an image file.
Wordpad Document	Creates a WordPad document.
Rich Text Document	Creates a document that can contain formatting.
Text Document	Creates a document that cannot contain any formatting.
Wave Sound	Creates a sound file.
Compressed (zipped) Folder	Creates a folder that compresses its contents to save storage space.

■ The new file appears with a temporary name.

5 Type a name for the new file and then press the **Enter** key.

*Note: A file name cannot contain the \ / : * ? " < > or | characters.*

CREATE A NEW FILE ON THE DESKTOP

1 Right-click a blank area on your desktop. A menu appears.

2 Click **New**.

3 Click the type of file you want to create.

4 Type a name for the new file and then press the **Enter** key.

CREATE A NEW FOLDER

You can create a new folder to help you organize the files stored on your computer.

Creating a folder is like placing a new folder in a filing cabinet.

CREATE A NEW FOLDER

1 Display the contents of the folder you want to contain a new folder.

Note: To browse through the folders on your computer, see pages 22 to 25.

2 Click **Make a new folder**.

Note: If the Make a new folder option is not available, click a blank area in the window to display the option.

■ The new folder appears, displaying a temporary name.

3 Type a name for the new folder and then press the `Enter` key.

*Note: A folder name cannot contain the \ / : * ? " < > or | characters.*

SIMPLIFY IT

How can creating a new folder help me organize the files on my computer?

You can create a new folder to store files you want to keep together, such as files for a particular project. This allows you to quickly locate the files. For example, you can create a folder named "Reports" that stores all of your reports. You can create as many folders as you need to set up a filing system that makes sense to you.

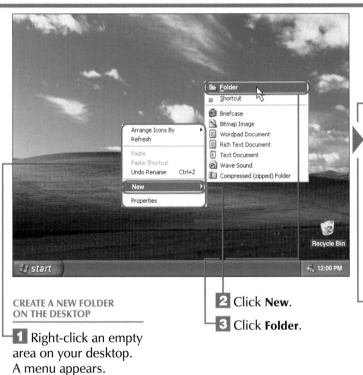

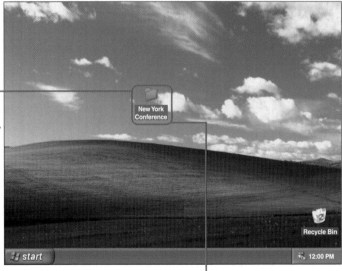

CREATE A NEW FOLDER ON THE DESKTOP

1 Right-click an empty area on your desktop. A menu appears.

2 Click **New**.

3 Click **Folder**.

■ The new folder appears, displaying a temporary name.

4 Type a name for the new folder and then press the Enter key.

*Note: A folder name cannot contain the \ / : * ? " < > or | characters.*

63

SEARCH FOR FILES

If you cannot remember the exact name or location of a file you want to work with, you can have Windows search for the file on your computer.

SEARCH FOR FILES

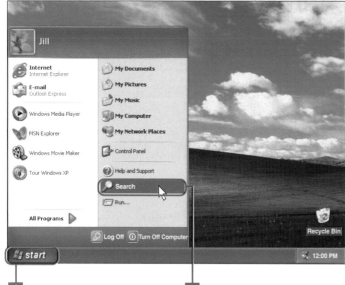

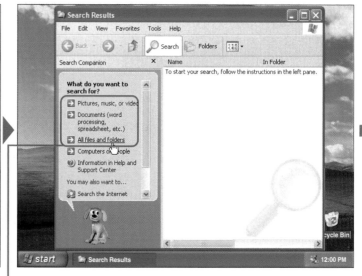

1 Click **start** to display the Start menu.

2 Click **Search** to search for files on your computer.

■ The Search Results window appears.

3 Click the type of file you want to search for.

*Note: The following options depend on the type of file you select. In this example, **All files and folders** is selected.*

What other options does Windows offer
to help me find a file?

Windows offers different options, depending on
the type of file you select in step 3 on page 64.

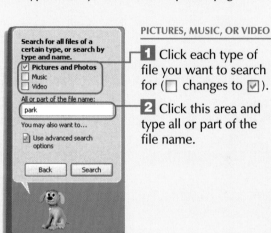

PICTURES, MUSIC, OR VIDEO

1 Click each type of
file you want to search
for (☐ changes to ☑).

2 Click this area and
type all or part of the
file name.

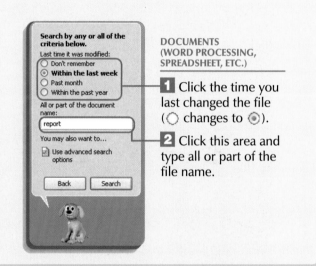

DOCUMENTS
(WORD PROCESSING,
SPREADSHEET, ETC.)

1 Click the time you
last changed the file
(○ changes to ◉).

2 Click this area and
type all or part of the
file name.

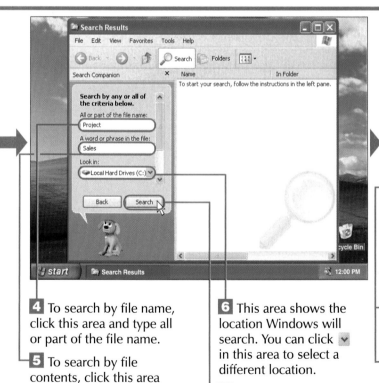

4 To search by file name,
click this area and type all
or part of the file name.

5 To search by file
contents, click this area
and type a word or phrase
that appears within the file.

6 This area shows the
location Windows will
search. You can click ▾
in this area to select a
different location.

7 Click **Search** to start
the search.

■ This area displays
the matching files that
Windows found.

■ To open a file,
double-click the file.

8 When you finish
viewing the results of
your search, click ☒
to close the Search
Results window.

You can add a shortcut to the desktop that will provide a quick way of opening a file you regularly use.

ADD A SHORTCUT TO THE DESKTOP

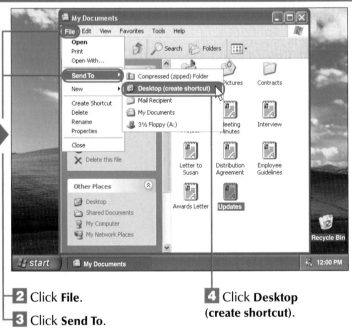

1 Click the file you want to create a shortcut to.

2 Click **File**.

3 Click **Send To**.

4 Click **Desktop (create shortcut)**.

How do I rename or delete a shortcut?

You can rename or delete a shortcut the same way you would rename or delete any file. Renaming or deleting a shortcut will not affect the original file. To rename a file, see page 37. To delete a file, see page 44.

Can I move a shortcut to a different location?

Yes. If you do not want a shortcut to appear on your desktop, you can move the shortcut to a different location on your computer. You can move a shortcut the same way you would move any file. To move a file, see page 48.

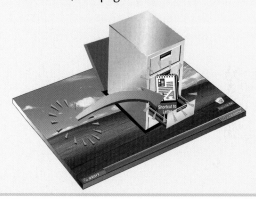

■ The shortcut appears on your desktop.

■ You can tell the difference between the shortcut and the original file because the shortcut icon displays an arrow (⤤).

■ You can double-click the shortcut to open the file at any time.

Note: You can create a shortcut to a folder the same way you create a shortcut to a file. Creating a shortcut to a folder will give you quick access to all the files in the folder.

COPY A FILE TO A FLOPPY DISK

You can copy a file stored on your computer to a floppy disk. This is useful if you want to give a friend, family member or colleague a copy of the file.

When copying a file to a floppy disk, you must use a formatted floppy disk.

COPY A FILE TO A FLOPPY DISK

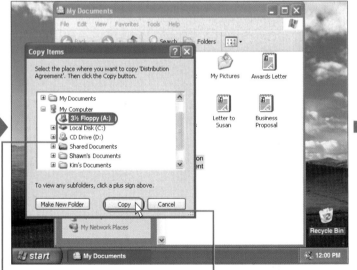

1 Insert a floppy disk into your floppy drive.

2 Click the file you want to copy to the floppy disk.

■ To copy more than one file, select all the files you want to copy. To select multiple files, see page 34.

3 Click **Copy this file**.

*Note: If you selected multiple files, click **Copy the selected items** in step 3.*

■ The Copy Items dialog box appears.

4 Click the drive that contains the floppy disk.

5 Click **Copy** to copy the file to the floppy disk.

How can I protect the information on my floppy disks?

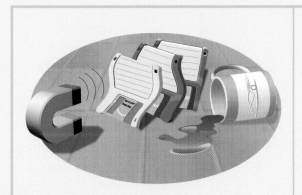  

not write-protected

write-protected

Store in a Safe Location

You should keep floppy disks away from moisture, heat and magnets, which can damage the information stored on the disks.

Write-protect

You can prevent people from making changes to information on floppy disks by sliding the tab on the disks to the write-protected position.

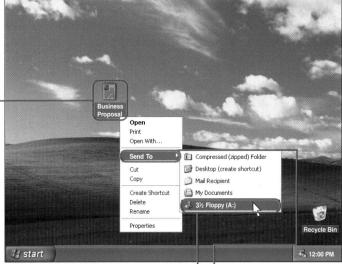

■ Windows places a copy of the file on the floppy disk.

Note: To view the contents of a floppy disk, see page 24.

■ You can copy a folder to a floppy disk the same way you copy a file. When you copy a folder, Windows copies all the files in the folder.

COPY A FILE ON YOUR DESKTOP

1 Insert a floppy disk into your floppy drive.

2 Right-click the file you want to copy to the floppy disk. A menu appears.

3 Click **Send To**.

4 Click the drive that contains the floppy disk.

You can copy files, such as documents and pictures, from your computer to a CD.

You will need a recordable CD drive to copy files to a CD. For information on recordable CD drives, see the top of page 95.

If you only want to copy songs to a CD, see page 94 for information on using Windows Media Player to copy the songs.

A CD can typically store 650 MB of information.

COPY FILES TO A CD

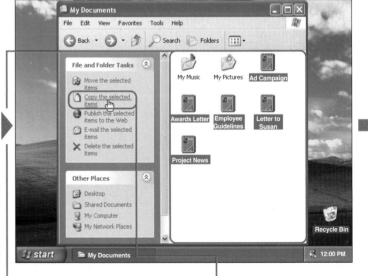

SELECT FILES TO COPY

1 Insert a CD into your recordable CD drive.

■ A dialog box may appear, asking what you want Windows to do.

2 Click **Take no action**.

3 Click **OK**.

Note: A window displaying the contents of the CD may appear instead of the dialog box. You can click ☒ in the window to close the window.

4 Select the files you want to copy to the CD. To select multiple files, see page 34.

5 Click **Copy the selected items**.

*Note: If you selected only one file, click **Copy this file** in step **5**.*

Why would I copy files to a CD?

You can copy files to a CD to transfer large amounts of information between computers or make backup copies of the files stored on your computer. Making backup copies of your files will provide you with extra copies of your files in case you accidentally erase the files or your computer fails.

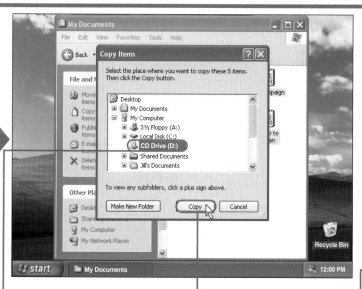

Can I copy a folder to a CD?

Yes. You can copy a folder to a CD the same way you copy files to a CD. When you copy a folder to a CD, Windows will copy all the files in the folder. To copy a folder to a CD, perform steps **1** to **7** starting on page 70, except select **Copy this folder** in step **5**. Then perform steps **1** to **8** starting on page 71.

■ The Copy Items dialog box appears.

6 Click the recordable CD drive that contains the CD you want to copy the files to.

7 Click **Copy** to place a copy of the files in a temporary storage area on your computer where the files will be held until you copy them to the CD.

■ You can repeat steps **4** to **7** for each set of files you want to copy to the CD.

COPY SELECTED FILES TO A CD

1 Click **start** to display the Start menu.

2 Click **My Computer** to view the contents of your computer.

CONTINUED

COPY FILES TO A CD

Before copying the files you selected to a CD, Windows stores the files in a temporary storage area on your computer. This allows you to review the files you selected before copying the files to a CD.

COPY FILES TO A CD (CONTINUED)

■ The My Computer window appears.

3 Double-click the recordable CD drive that contains the CD you want to copy the files to.

■ A window appears, displaying the files being held in a temporary storage area on your computer and any files currently stored on the CD.

Note: If the window displays a file you no longer want to copy to the CD, you can delete the file. To delete a file, see page 44.

4 Click **Write these files to CD** to copy the files to the CD.

Can I copy files to a CD at different times?

Yes. Each time you copy files to a CD, however, approximately 20 MB of extra information is stored on the CD. To make the best use of the storage space on the CD, you may want to copy all the files to the CD at one time.

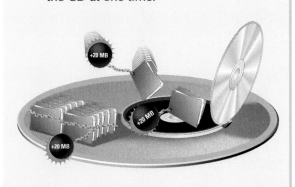

How do I erase a CD-RW disc?

You can erase a CD-RW disc to permanently delete all the files on the disc. You cannot erase a CD-R disc.

2 Click **Erase this CD-RW**.

■ The CD Writing Wizard appears. Follow the instructions in the wizard to erase the disc.

1 Display the contents of your CD-RW disc. To view the contents of a CD, see page 24.

■ The CD Writing Wizard appears.

5 Type a name for the CD.

Note: The name you specify for the CD will appear in the My Computer window when the CD is in a CD drive. To view the My Computer window, see page 24.

6 Click **Next** to copy the files to the CD.

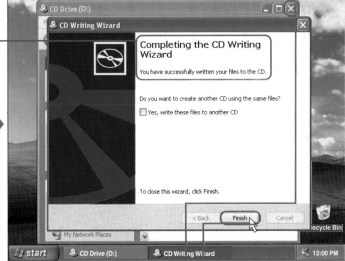

■ This message appears when Windows has successfully copied the files to the CD.

Note: Windows will automatically eject the CD from your recordable CD drive when the copy is complete.

7 Click **Finish** to close the wizard.

8 Click ✕ to close the window for the recordable CD drive.

Note: To display the contents of a CD to confirm that the files were copied, see page 24.

CHAPTER 4

WORK WITH MUSIC AND VIDEOS

In this chapter, you will learn how to use the Windows Media Player program. You will find out how to play music CDs, listen to radio stations on the Internet, copy songs to a CD or portable device and more.

You can use Windows Media Player to play many types of sound and video files on your computer.

You can obtain sound and video files on the Internet and purchase sound and video files at computer stores.

PLAY A SOUND OR VIDEO

1 Double-click the sound or video file you want to play.

■ The Windows Media Player window appears.

■ If you selected a video file, this area displays the video.

Note: If you selected a sound file, the sound plays. The area may display a graphical representation of the sound.

■ This slider (🔘) indicates the progress of the sound or video file.

2 To use the entire screen to view the video that is currently playing, click 🔲.

SIMPLIFY IT

Can I display Windows Media Player in a smaller size?

Yes. You can change the size and appearance of Windows Media Player by switching from the full mode to the skin mode.

Full Mode

The full mode allows you to access all the features that Windows Media Player provides. You can click to switch to the skin mode at any time.

Skin Mode

The skin mode takes up less room on your screen, but offers fewer features than the full mode. You can click to return to the full mode at any time.

■ The video continues to play using the entire screen.

■ To once again display the video in a window, press the Esc key.

3 To adjust the volume, drag this slider ( ) left or right to decrease or increase the volume.

4 To pause or stop the play of the sound or video file, click or (changes to).

■ You can click to resume the play of the sound or video file.

5 When you finish playing the sound or video file, click to close the Windows Media Player window.

77

You can use your computer to play music CDs while you work.

You need a computer with sound capabilities and a CD-ROM drive to play music CDs.

PLAY A MUSIC CD

1 Insert a music CD into your CD-ROM drive.

■ The Audio CD dialog box appears, asking what you want Windows to do.

2 Click this option to play the music CD.

3 Click **OK**.

■ The Windows Media Player window appears and the CD begins to play.

■ This area displays a graphical representation of the song that is currently playing.

How does Windows Media Player
know the name of each song on
my music CD?

If you are connected to the Internet when
you play a music CD, Windows Media
Player attempts to obtain information
about the CD from the Internet. If you
are not connected to the Internet or
information about the CD is unavailable,
Windows Media Player displays the track
number of each song instead. If Windows
Media Player is able to obtain information
about the CD, Windows will recognize
the CD and display the appropriate
information each time you insert the CD.

■ This area displays a list
of the songs on the CD
and the amount of time
that each song will play.
The song that is currently
playing is highlighted.

■ This slider ( )
indicates the progress
of the current song.

■ This area displays
the amount of time the
current song has been
playing.

ADJUST THE VOLUME

4 To adjust the
volume, drag this
slider ( ) left or
right to decrease or
increase the volume.

TURN OFF SOUND

5 Click 📢 to turn off the
sound (📢 changes to 🔇).

■ You can click 🔇 to once
again turn on the sound.

CONTINUED

When playing a music CD, you can pause or stop the play of the CD at any time. You can also play a specific song or play the songs in random order.

PLAY A MUSIC CD (CONTINUED)

PAUSE OR STOP PLAY

6 Click (⏸) to pause the play of the CD (⏸ changes to ▶).

7 Click (⏹) to stop the play of the CD.

■ You can click (▶) to resume the play of the CD.

PLAY ANOTHER SONG

■ This area displays a list of the songs on the CD.

8 Click one of the following options to play another song on the CD.

(◀◀) Play the previous song

(▶▶) Play the next song

■ To play a specific song in the list, double-click the song.

How can I play a music CD while performing other tasks on my computer?

If you want to perform other tasks on your computer while playing a music CD, minimize the Windows Media Player window to temporarily remove the window from your screen. To minimize the Windows Media Player window, click ━ in the top right corner of the window.

Can I listen to a music CD privately?

You can listen to a music CD privately by plugging headphones into the jack at the front of your CD-ROM drive or into your speakers. If your CD-ROM drive or speakers do not have a headphone jack, you can plug the headphones into the back of your computer where you normally plug in the speakers.

PLAY SONGS RANDOMLY

9 Click 🔀 to play the songs on the CD in random order (🔀 changes to 🔀).

■ You can click 🔀 to once again play the songs on the CD in order.

CLOSE WINDOWS MEDIA PLAYER

10 When you finish listening to the CD, click ✖ to close the Windows Media Player window.

11 Remove the CD from your CD-ROM drive.

USING THE MEDIA GUIDE

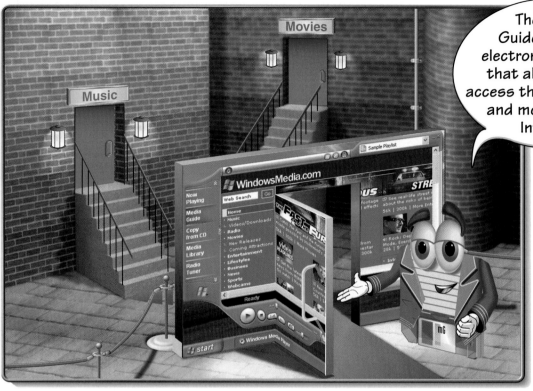

The Media Guide is like an electronic magazine that allows you to access the latest music and movies on the Internet.

You can also use the Media Guide to obtain information on various topics such as news, sports and entertainment.

You must have a connection to the Internet to use the Media Guide.

USING THE MEDIA GUIDE

1 Click **start** to display the Start menu.

2 Click **All Programs** to view a list of the programs on your computer.

3 Click **Windows Media Player**.

■ The Windows Media Player window appears.

4 Click the **Media Guide** tab.

Note: If you are not currently connected to the Internet, a message appears, indicating that you need to be connected.

■ This area displays the Media Guide, which is a Web page that is updated daily to provide access to the latest music, movies and information on the Internet.

Note: The Media Guide may look different on your screen.

Why are different speeds listed for a media file in the Media Guide?

The Media Guide offers files for different connection speeds that you can select to transfer and play a media file such as a music video or movie clip. The connection speed you should select depends on the type of connection you have to the Internet. If problems occur while transferring or playing a media file, try selecting a slower connection speed.

Type of Connection	Select this Speed
Modem	28k or 56k
Integrated Services Digital Network (ISDN) Line	100k
Cable Modem or Digital Subscriber Line (DSL) Modem	300k or 500k

■ The Media Guide contains links that you can click to display additional information or play media files such as music videos or movie clips. When you position the mouse ⩗ over a link, the mouse ⩗ changes to 🖑.

5 Click a link of interest.

■ In this example, information on the topic you selected appears.

■ You can repeat step **5** to browse through additional information or play other media files.

6 When you finish using the Media Guide, click ✖ to close the Windows Media Player window.

You can use the Media Library to organize and work with all the media files on your computer. A media file can be a sound or video file.

USING THE MEDIA LIBRARY

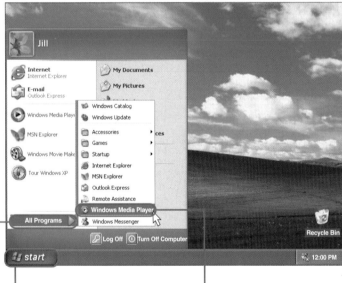

1 Click **start** to display the Start menu.

2 Click **All Programs** to view a list of the programs on your computer.

3 Click **Windows Media Player**.

■ The Windows Media Player window appears.

4 Click the **Media Library** tab.

■ The first time you visit the Media Library, a dialog box appears, asking if you want to search your computer for media files.

5 Click **Yes** to search your computer for media files.

Note: If the dialog box does not appear, press the **F3** *key to search your computer for media files.*

SIMPLIFY IT

Where can I obtain media files?

Media Guide

You can use the Media Guide that Windows provides to access the latest music, movies and videos on the Internet. For more information on the Media Guide, see page 82.

The Internet

Many Web sites on the Internet offer media files that you can transfer and play on your computer. You can find media files at the following Web sites.
earthstation1.com
www.themez.co.uk

Computer Stores

Many computer stores offer collections of media files that you can purchase.

■ The Search for Media Files dialog box appears.

6 Click **Search** to start the search.

■ Windows searches your computer for media files.

■ This area shows the progress of the search.

7 When the search is complete, click **Close** to close the dialog box.

8 Click **Close** to close the Search for Media Files dialog box.

CONTINUED

USING THE MEDIA LIBRARY

You can play sound and video files that are listed in the Media Library.

USING THE MEDIA LIBRARY (CONTINUED)

VIEW MEDIA FILES

■ The Media Library organizes your media files into categories.

■ A category displaying a plus sign (➕) contains hidden items.

■ To display the hidden items in a category, click the plus sign (➕) beside the category (➕ changes to ➖).

Note: To once again hide the items in a category, click the minus sign (➖) beside the category.

1 Click the category that contains the media files of interest.

■ This area displays the media files in the category you selected.

2 To play a media file, double-click the file.

How does the Media Library organize my sound and video files?

The Media Library organizes your sound and video files into the following categories.

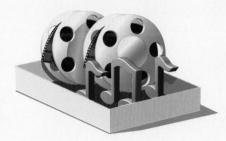

AUDIO

All Audio	Lists all your sound files.
Album	Lists sound files by album.
Artist	Lists sound files by artist.
Genre	Lists sound files by genre, such as Jazz or Rock.

VIDEO

All Clips	Lists all your video files.
Author	Lists video files by author.

■ If you selected a video file, the video appears on the **Now Playing** tab.

■ This slider (🔘) indicates the progress of the video or sound file.

3 To adjust the volume, drag this slider (🔘) left or right to decrease or increase the volume.

4 To stop playing the video or sound file, click 🔘.

■ To return to your list of media files, click the **Media Library** tab.

5 When you finish working with your media files, click ✖ to close the Windows Media Player window.

You can use Windows Media Player to listen to radio stations from around the world that broadcast on the Internet.

You need a computer with sound capabilities and an Internet connection to listen to radio stations that broadcast on the Internet.

LISTEN TO RADIO STATIONS ON THE INTERNET

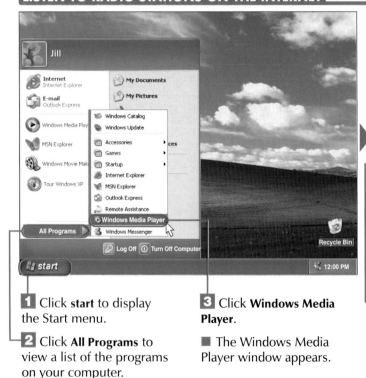

1 Click **start** to display the Start menu.

2 Click **All Programs** to view a list of the programs on your computer.

3 Click **Windows Media Player**.

■ The Windows Media Player window appears.

4 Click the **Radio Tuner** tab to listen to radio stations that broadcast on the Internet.

Note: If you are not currently connected to the Internet, a message appears, indicating that you need to be connected.

■ This area displays a list of featured radio stations.

5 Click the name of the radio station you want to play.

How does Windows play radio stations that broadcast on the Internet?

Before Windows plays a radio station, the information is partially transferred and temporarily stored in a section of memory on your computer, called a buffer. While the radio station plays, information continuously transfers from the Internet and is temporarily stored in the buffer. The buffer minimizes the interruptions to the broadcast playing on your computer. Interruptions are caused by disruptions to information or the slowing down of information transferring to your computer.

■ Information about the radio station you selected appears.

6 Click **Play** to play the radio station.

Note: If the Play option is not available, see the top of page 91.

■ After a moment, the radio station begins to play.

■ The Microsoft Internet Explorer window opens behind Windows Media Player, displaying the Web page for the radio station. To clearly view the Web page, click the window's button on the taskbar.

7 To adjust the volume, drag the slider ( ) left or right to decrease or increase the volume.

8 To stop playing the radio station at any time, click .

CONTINUED ➤

You can search for radio stations that broadcast on the Internet.

LISTEN TO RADIO STATIONS ON THE INTERNET (CONTINUED)

SEARCH FOR RADIO STATIONS

■ This area displays categories of radio stations you can search for.

1 To search for radio stations in a specific category, click the category of interest.

■ A list of radio stations in the category you selected appears.

■ If the radio station you want to listen to does not appear in the list, you can click this area and type a word or phrase that describes the radio station you want to search for. Then press the Enter key.

2 Click the name of the radio station that you want to play in the list.

How do I listen to a radio station
if the Play option is not available?

If the Play option does not appear when
you click the name of a radio station,
you cannot listen to the radio station in
Windows Media Player. To listen to the
radio station using your Web browser,
click the **Visit Website to Play** option. A
Web browser window opens, displaying
the Web page for the radio station and
the radio station begins playing. Some
radio stations may require additional
information before allowing you to listen
to the station in your Web browser.

■ Information about the
radio station you selected
appears.

*Note: If the Play option is
not available, see the top
of this page.*

3 Click **Play** to play the
radio station.

■ After a moment, the radio
station begins to play.

■ The Microsoft Internet
Explorer window opens
behind Windows Media Player,
displaying the Web page for
the radio station. To clearly
view the Web page, click the
window's button on the taskbar.

4 When you finish
listening to radio stations,
click ✖ to close the
Windows Media Player
window.

You can copy songs from a music CD onto your computer.

Copying songs from a music CD allows you to play the songs at any time without having to insert the CD into your computer. Copying songs from a music CD also allows you to later copy the songs to a recordable CD or portable device.

Your CD-ROM drive and speakers determine whether you can listen to a music CD while you copy songs from the CD.

COPY SONGS FROM A MUSIC CD

1 Insert the music CD that contains the songs you want to copy into your CD-ROM drive.

■ The Audio CD dialog box appears, asking what you want Windows to do.

2 Click this option to play the music CD.

3 Click **OK**.

■ The Windows Media Player window appears and the CD begins to play.

4 Click the **Copy from CD** tab.

■ This area displays information about each song on the CD. Windows Media Player will copy each song that displays a check mark (✔) to your computer.

5 To add (✔) or remove (☐) a check mark beside a song, click the box (☐) beside the song.

6 Click **Copy Music** to start copying the selected songs to your computer.

92

How can I play a song I copied from a music CD?

Windows offers two ways that you can play a song you copied from a music CD.

Use the My Music Folder

Songs you copy from a music CD are stored in the My Music folder on your computer. The My Music folder contains a subfolder for each artist whose songs you have copied to your computer. To open the My Music folder, see page 23. You can double-click a song in the folder to play the song.

Use Windows Media Player

Songs you copy from a music CD are listed in the Media Library in Windows Media Player. To play a song in the Media Library, see page 84.

■ The first time you copy songs from a music CD, a dialog box appears, stating that Windows Media Player will protect the songs from unauthorized use. Protected songs cannot be played on another computer.

7 If you want to be able to play the songs on another computer, click this option (☐ changes to ☑).

8 Click **OK** to continue.

■ This column indicates the progress of the copy.

■ To stop the copy at any time, click **Stop Copy**.

9 When you finish copying songs from the music CD, click ✖ to close the Windows Media Player window.

You can use Windows Media Player to copy songs on your computer to a CD or to a portable device such as an MP3 player.

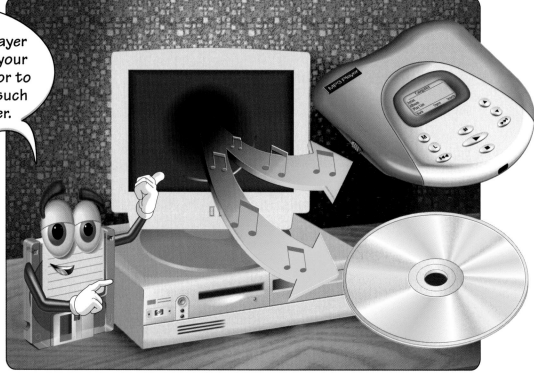

When using Windows Media Player to copy songs, you can only copy songs that appear in the Media Library. For information on using the Media Library, see page 84. To add songs to the Media Library from a music CD, see page 92.

You should not perform other tasks on your computer when copying songs to a CD since Windows Media Player may stop working.

COPY SONGS TO A CD OR PORTABLE DEVICE

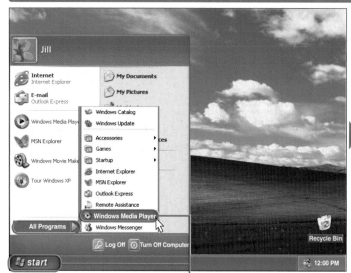

1 To copy songs to a CD, insert a blank CD into your recordable CD drive.

*Note: When you insert a blank CD, a dialog box appears, asking what you want Windows to do. Click **Cancel** to close the dialog box.*

2 Click **start** to display the Start menu.

3 Click **All Programs** to view a list of the programs on your computer.

4 Click **Windows Media Player**.

■ The Windows Media Player window appears.

5 Click the **Copy to CD or Device** tab.

■ If the Copy to CD or Device tab is not displayed, click this arrow (☒) until the tab appears.

6 Click this area to display a list of the categories in the Media Library.

7 Click the category that contains the songs you want to copy.

94

What hardware do I need to copy songs to a CD?

You will need a recordable CD drive to copy songs to a CD.

CD-R Drive

A CD-R (Compact Disc-Recordable) drive allows you to permanently record data on CD-R discs. You cannot erase the contents of a CD-R disc.

CD-RW Drive

A CD-RW (Compact Disc-ReWritable) drive allows you to record data on CD-RW or CD-R discs. You can erase the contents of a CD-RW disc in order to copy new data to the disc. To erase the contents of a CD-RW disc, see the top of page 73.

Can I copy songs to a CD at different times?

You can copy songs to a CD only once using Windows Media Player. Since you must copy all the songs to a CD at the same time, make sure you carefully select all the songs you want to copy.

■ This area displays the songs in the category you selected. Windows Media Player will copy each song that displays a check mark (✔).

8 To add (☑) or remove (☐) a check mark, click the box (☐) beside the song.

■ This area displays the device you will copy the songs to. You can click this area to select a different device.

9 Click **Copy Music** to start copying.

■ This column indicates the progress of the copy.

■ To cancel the copy at any time, click **Cancel**.

■ When the copy is complete, this area displays all the songs you copied to the device.

Note: When you copy songs to a CD, Windows automatically ejects the CD from the recordable CD drive when the copy is complete.

10 Click ✖ to close the Windows Media Player window.

CHAPTER 5

CREATE MOVIES

Read this chapter to find out how to use the Windows Movie Maker program. You will learn how to record, play and edit your own home movies.

You can use Windows Movie Maker to transfer your home movies to your computer. You can then organize and edit the movies before sharing them with friends and family.

Before using Windows Movie Maker, you need to connect and install the equipment needed to transfer your home movies to your computer.

Video Source

You can transfer movies from a video camera onto your computer. You can also transfer movies from a Web camera, television broadcast, VCR or DVD player onto your computer.

Cables

You will need one or more cables to connect the video camera or other video source to your computer. The video source or the card you use to connect the video source to your computer may come with the cables you need. If you do not have the required cables, you can purchase the cables at a computer store.

Connector

You need a specific type of connector to be able to connect a video camera or other video source to your computer. If your computer does not already have the appropriate type of connector, you can purchase the connector at a computer store.

Video Source	Type of Connector Commonly Required
Analog Video Camera	Video Capture Card
Digital Video Camera	FireWire Port or FireWire Card
DVD	TV Tuner Card
Television Broadcast	TV Tuner Card
VCR	TV Tuner Card
Web Camera	USB Port or USB Card

Minimum Computer Requirements

Your computer must have the following minimum requirements for Windows Movie Maker to work properly.

➤ 400 MHz Pentium II or equivalent

➤ 128 MB of RAM

➤ 2 GB of free hard disk space

➤ Sound capabilities

START WINDOWS MOVIE MAKER

You can start Windows Movie Maker to create and work with movies on your computer.

START WINDOWS MOVIE MAKER

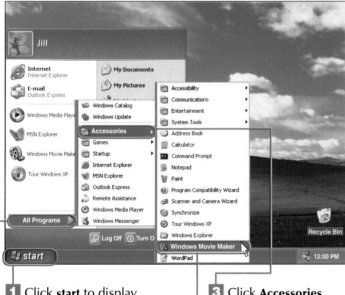

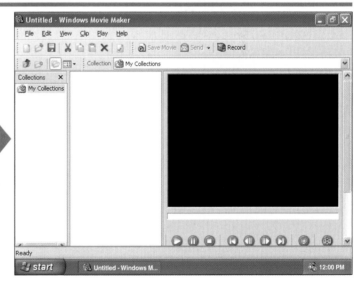

1 Click **start** to display the Start menu.

2 Click **All Programs** to view a list of the programs on your computer.

3 Click **Accessories**.

4 Click **Windows Movie Maker**.

■ The Windows Movie Maker window appears.

■ You can now record video from your video camera or other video source onto your computer. To record video onto your computer, see page 100.

RECORD A VIDEO

You can record video from your video camera or other video source onto your computer.

Before you start recording video, make sure your video camera or other video source is properly connected to your computer and turned on. Also make sure the tape or other media is at the point where you want to begin recording.

RECORD A VIDEO

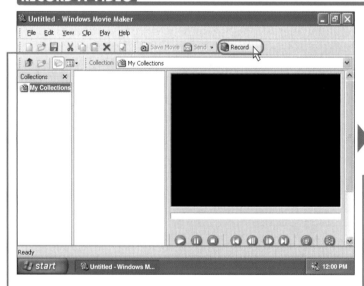

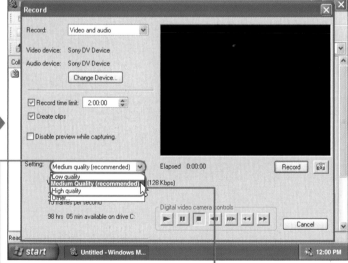

1 Click **Record** to record a video onto your computer.

*Note: A dialog box appears if your computer may not provide acceptable performance when recording from a high-speed device such as a digital video camera. Click **Yes** to record video using the device.*

■ The Record dialog box appears.

2 Click this area to display a list of the available quality settings that you can use to record the video.

3 Click the quality setting you want to use.

Note: For information on selecting a quality setting, see the top of page 101.

Why am I unable to record video from my video camera?

When recording video from a video camera, make sure your camera is in Playback mode and not in Standby mode. You cannot record video when your video camera is in Standby mode.

What should I consider when selecting a quality setting to record my video?

A higher quality setting produces a higher quality video, but results in a larger file size. Videos with a larger file size take up more space on your computer and will take longer to transfer over the Internet. Some computers also may not be able to properly play a higher quality video.

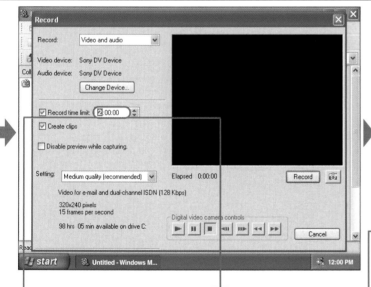

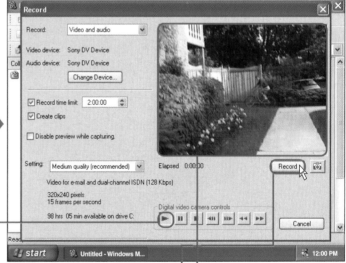

■ This area indicates the time period after which Windows Movie Maker will stop recording the video.

Note: The default recording time is set at two hours. The time may be less, depending on your free hard disk space and the quality setting you select in step 3.

4 To change the length of time, click the part of the time you want to change and then type a new number.

5 Click ▶ to begin playing the video.

Note: You can also press the play button on your video camera or other video source to begin playing the video.

■ This area displays the video.

6 Click **Record** to start recording the video onto your computer.

CONTINUED ▶

RECORD A VIDEO

Windows automatically stores each video you record in the My Videos folder on your computer.

Windows creates the My Videos folder the first time you start Windows Movie Maker. The My Videos folder is stored within the My Documents folder.

RECORD A VIDEO (CONTINUED)

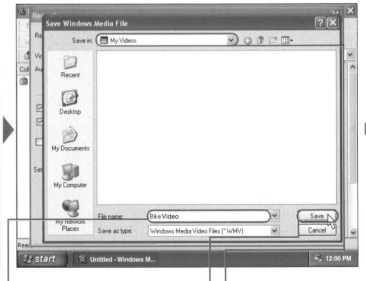

■ The word **Recording** blinks in this area when you are recording.

■ This area displays the time that has passed since you started recording the video.

7 Click **Stop** when you want to stop recording the video.

Note: You may have to press the stop button on your video camera or other video source to stop the video.

■ The Save Windows Media File dialog box appears.

8 Type a name for your video.

■ This area shows the location where Windows Movie Maker will store your video. You can click this area to change the location.

9 Click **Save** to save the video.

How does Windows Movie Maker organize the videos I record?

Collections

Each time you record a video, Windows Movie Maker creates a collection to store all the clips for the video. Each collection appears as a folder (📁) in the Windows Movie Maker window.

Clips

Windows Movie Maker automatically breaks up a video you record into smaller, more manageable segments, called clips. A clip is created each time Windows detects a different sequence in a video, such as when you turn on your video camera or when you switch from pause to once again begin recording.

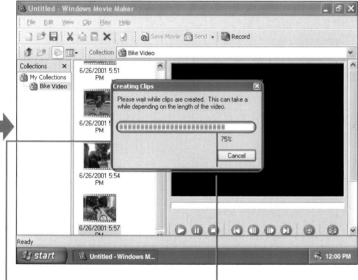

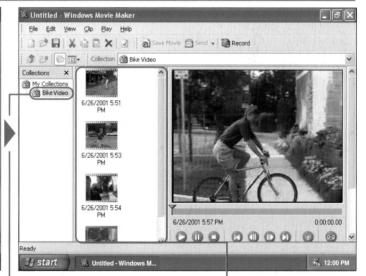

■ The Creating Clips dialog box appears while Windows Movie Maker creates the clips for your video. For information on clips, see the top of this page.

■ This area shows the progress of the creation of the clips.

■ When Windows Movie Maker has finished creating the clips for your video, this area displays a folder that stores the collection of video clips. The name of the collection is the name you specified in step 8.

■ This area displays the video clips within the collection. To help you identify the video clips, Windows Movie Maker displays the first frame of each clip.

103

You can play each video clip that you have recorded on your computer.

Playing video clips can help you determine which clips you want to include in your movie.

PLAY A VIDEO CLIP

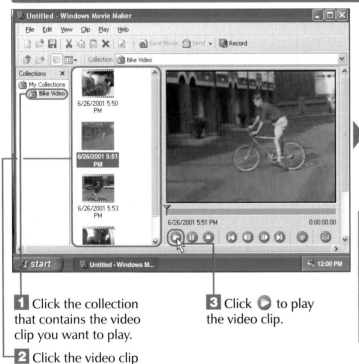

1 Click the collection that contains the video clip you want to play.

2 Click the video clip you want to play.

3 Click ▶ to play the video clip.

■ The video clip plays in this area.

■ This arrow (▽) indicates the progress of the video clip.

4 To pause or stop the video clip, click ⏸ or ⏹.

Note: To once again play the video clip, repeat steps 2 and 3.

You must add each video clip that you want to include in your movie to the storyboard.

The storyboard displays the order in which video clips will play in your movie.

ADD A VIDEO CLIP TO THE STORYBOARD

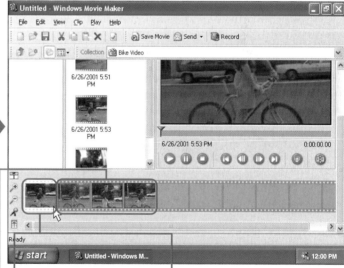

1 Click the collection that contains the video clip you want to add to the storyboard.

2 Click the video clip you want to add.

3 Click **Clip**.

4 Click **Add to Storyboard/Timeline**.

■ The video clip appears on the storyboard.

■ You can repeat steps **1** to **4** for each video clip you want to add to the storyboard.

REMOVE A VIDEO CLIP

1 Click the video clip on the storyboard that you want to remove. Then press the Delete key.

Note: Deleting a video clip from the storyboard will not remove the video clip from Windows Movie Maker.

105

You can change the order of the video clips on the storyboard to change the order in which the clips will play in your movie.

REARRANGE VIDEO CLIPS ON THE STORYBOARD

1 Position the mouse ⬚ over the video clip on the storyboard that you want to move to a different location.

2 Drag the video clip to a new location on the storyboard. A vertical bar indicates where the video clip will appear.

■ The video clip appears in the new location.

■ The surrounding video clips automatically move to make room for the video clip.

SAVE A PROJECT

You can save a project so you can later review and make changes to the project.

A project is a rough draft of your movie that contains all the video clips you added to the storyboard. You should regularly save changes you make to a project to avoid losing your work.

SAVE A PROJECT

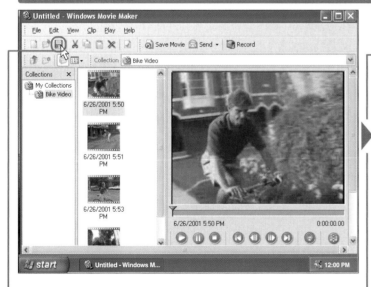

1 Click 💾 to save your project.

■ The Save Project dialog box appears.

Note: If you previously saved your project, the Save Project dialog box will not appear since you have already named the project.

2 Type a name for your project.

■ This area shows the location where Windows Movie Maker will store your project. You can click this area to change the location.

3 Click **Save** to save your project.

You can open a saved project to display the video clips in the project. Opening a project allows you to review and make changes to the project.

Bike Ride

A project is a rough draft of your movie that contains all the video clips you added to the storyboard.

You can only work with one project at a time. If you are currently working with a project, make sure you save the project before opening another project. To save a project, see page 107.

OPEN A PROJECT

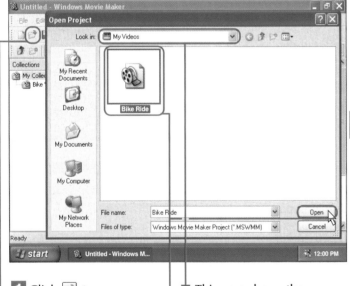

1 Click 📂 to open a project.

■ The Open Project dialog box appears.

■ This area shows the location of the displayed projects. You can click this area to change the location.

2 Click the name of the project you want to open.

3 Click **Open** to open the project.

■ The project opens and the video clips in the project appear on the storyboard. You can now review and make changes to the project.

PREVIEW A MOVIE

You can preview all the video clips you have added to the storyboard as a movie.

PREVIEW A MOVIE

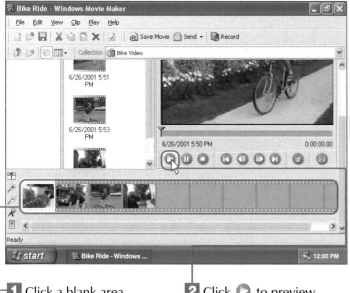

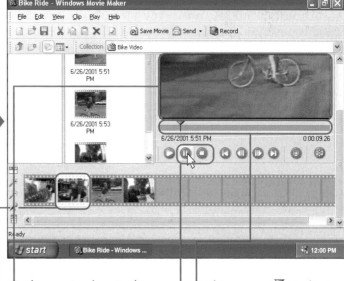

1 Click a blank area on the storyboard.

2 Click ▶ to preview all the video clips you have added to the storyboard as a movie.

■ The movie plays in this area.

■ A white border appears around the video clip that is currently playing.

■ This arrow (▼) indicates the progress of the movie.

3 To pause or stop the movie, click ⏸ or ⏹.

Note: To once again play the movie, click ▶.

After you add all the video clips that you want to include in your movie to the storyboard, you can save the movie on your computer.

Saving a movie allows you to play the movie at any time and share the movie with friends and family.

SAVE A MOVIE

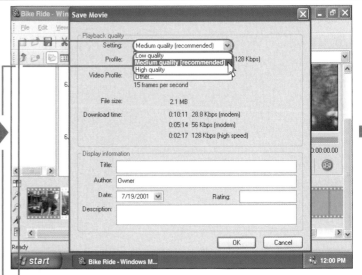

1 Click **Save Movie** to save the video clips on the storyboard as a movie.

■ The Save Movie dialog box appears.

2 Click this area to display a list of the quality settings that you can use for the movie.

3 Click the quality setting you want to use.

Note: Higher quality settings result in larger movie file sizes. Make sure you do not select a higher quality setting than you used to record your video.

How can I share a movie with friends and family?

Publish a Movie to the Web

You can publish a movie to the Web to allow people to view the movie. To publish a movie to the Web, see page 54.

Send a Movie in an E-mail Message

You can send a movie in an e-mail message. You should try to keep your movies under 2 MB (2,000 KB) since most companies that provide e-mail accounts limit the size of the messages that you can send and receive over the Internet. To send a movie in an e-mail message, see page 52.

Copy a Movie to a CD

If you have a recordable CD drive, you can copy a movie from your computer to a CD. You can then share the CD with other people. To copy a movie to a CD, see page 70.

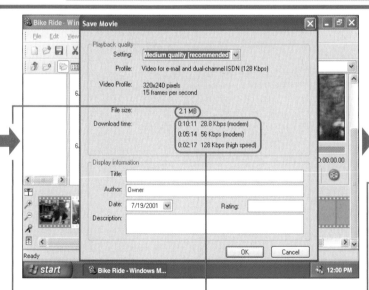

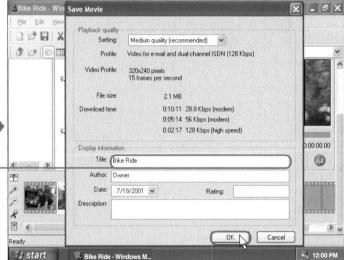

■ This area displays the file size of the movie.

■ This area displays the estimated amount of time the movie will take to transfer over the Internet using three different types of Internet connections.

4 Click this area and type a title for the movie.

Note: People who view your movie in Windows Media Player will be able to view the title you enter.

5 Click **OK** to continue.

CONTINUED

SAVE A MOVIE

After you save a movie on your computer, you can view the movie in Windows Media Player.

SAVE A MOVIE (CONTINUED)

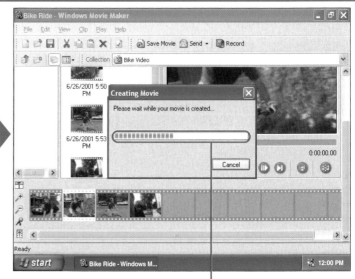

■ The Save As dialog box appears.

6 Type a name for the movie.

■ This area shows the location where Windows Movie Maker will store the movie. You can click this area to change the location.

7 Click **Save** to save the movie.

■ The Creating Movie dialog box appears while Windows Movie Maker creates your movie.

■ This area shows the progress of the creation of the movie.

SIMPLIFY IT

How can I later play a movie I have saved?

Windows automatically stores your movies in the My Videos folder, which is a subfolder within the My Documents folder. You can double-click a movie in the My Videos folder to play the movie. To view the contents of the My Documents folder, see page 22.

SIMPLIFY IT

Can I make changes to a movie I have saved?

No. You cannot make changes to a movie you have saved. Windows Movie Maker only allows you to make changes to a project, which is a rough draft of a movie. To open a project, see page 108.

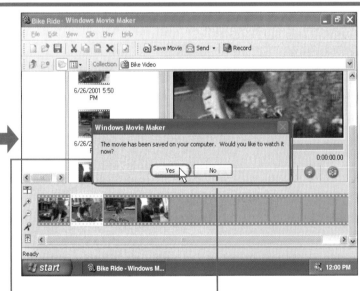

■ A dialog box appears when Windows Movie Maker has finished creating and saving your movie.

8 Click **Yes** to watch the movie now.

*Note: If you do not want to watch the movie now, click **No**.*

■ The Windows Media Player window appears.

■ The movie plays in this area.

9 To pause or stop the movie, click (❙❙) or (■) ((❙❙) changes to (▶)).

Note: To once again play the movie, click (▶).

10 When you finish viewing the movie, click ✖ to close the Windows Media Player window.

CHAPTER 6

SHARE YOUR COMPUTER

If you share your computer with one or more people, you can create user accounts so each person can use their own personalized files and settings. In this chapter, you will learn how to create and work with the user accounts on your computer.

CREATE A USER ACCOUNT

If you share your computer with other people, you can create a personalized user account for each person.

You must have a computer administrator account to create a user account. For information on the types of accounts, see page 118.

CREATE A USER ACCOUNT

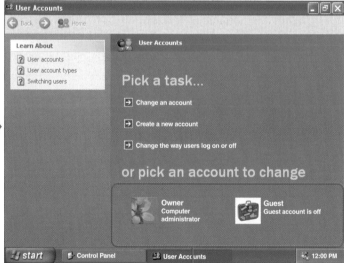

1 Click **start** to display the Start menu.

2 Click **Control Panel** to change your computer's settings.

■ The Control Panel window appears.

3 Click **User Accounts** to work with the user accounts set up on your computer.

■ The User Accounts window appears.

■ This area displays the user accounts that are currently set up on your computer.

Will Windows keep my personal files separate from the files of other users?

Yes. Windows will keep your personal files separate from the personal files created by other users. For example, your My Documents folder displays only the files you have created.

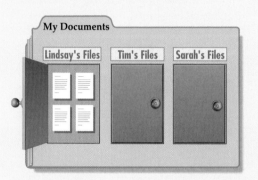

How can I personalize Windows for my user account?

You can personalize the appearance of Windows for your user account by changing the screen saver, desktop background and many other computer settings.

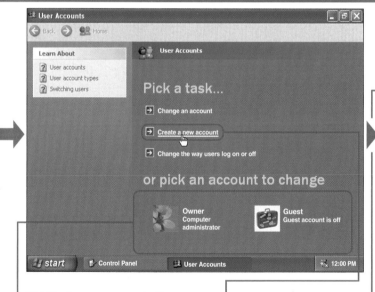

■ Windows automatically creates the Owner and Guest accounts on your computer.

■ The Owner account is a computer administrator account. The Guest account allows a person without a user account to use the computer.

Note: If user accounts were created when Windows was installed on your computer, the first user account created replaced the Owner account.

4 Click **Create a new account**.

5 Type a name for the new account.

Note: The name will appear on the Welcome screen when you log on to Windows and at the top of your Start menu.

6 Click **Next** to continue.

CONTINUED

CREATE A USER ACCOUNT

When you create a user account, you must select the type of account you want to create.

Computer Administrator

The user can perform any task on the computer. For example, the user can create and change all user accounts as well as install programs and hardware.

Limited

The user can perform only certain tasks on the computer. For example, the user can create and change their own password and change some computer settings but cannot delete important files.

CREATE A USER ACCOUNT (CONTINUED)

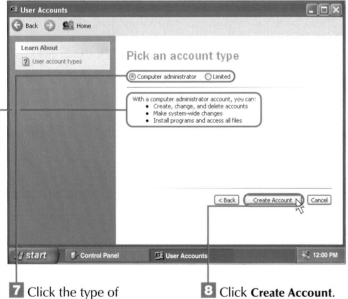

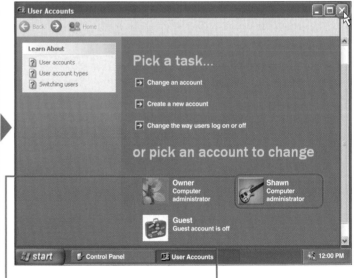

7 Click the type of account you want to create (○ changes to ◉).

■ This area displays a description of the account type you selected.

8 Click **Create Account**.

■ This area displays the account you created.

9 Click ✖ to close the User Accounts window.

118

DELETE A USER ACCOUNT

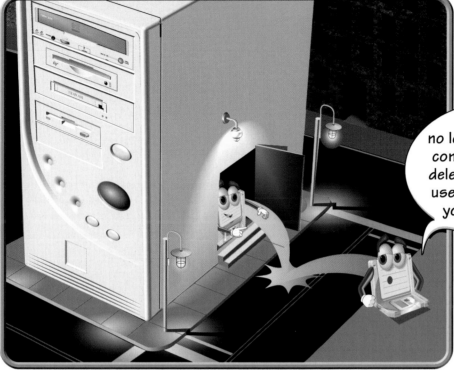

If a person no longer uses your computer, you can delete the person's user account from your computer.

You must have a computer administrator account to delete a user account. For information on the types of accounts, see page 118.

DELETE A USER ACCOUNT

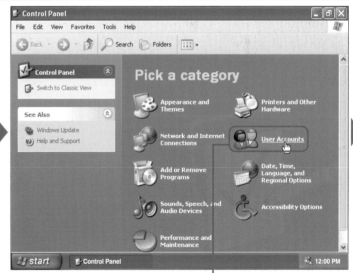

1 Click **start** to display the Start menu.

2 Click **Control Panel** to change your computer's settings.

■ The Control Panel window appears.

3 Click **User Accounts** to work with the user accounts set up on your computer.

CONTINUED

DELETE A USER ACCOUNT

When you delete a user account, you can choose to keep or delete the user's personal files.

If you choose to delete a user's personal files, Windows will permanently delete the files from your computer.

DELETE A USER ACCOUNT (CONTINUED)

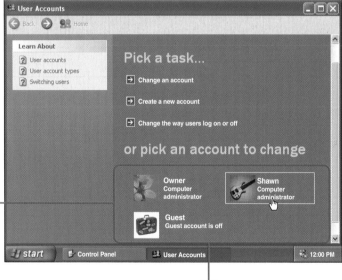

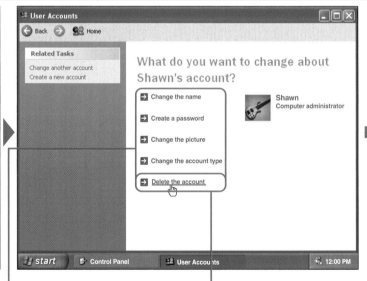

■ The User Accounts window appears.

■ This area displays the accounts that are set up on your computer.

4 Click the account you want to delete.

Note: You cannot delete the Guest account, which allows a person without a user account to use your computer.

■ A list of tasks that you can perform to change the user account appears.

5 Click **Delete the account**.

If I choose to keep the personal files for a deleted user account, which files will Windows save?

Windows will save the user's personal files that are displayed on the desktop and stored in the My Documents folder. The files will be saved on your desktop in a new folder that has the same name as the deleted account. Windows will not save the user's e-mail messages, list of favorite Web pages and other computer settings.

Can I delete a computer administrator account?

Yes. If you have a computer administrator account, you can delete other computer administrator accounts. Windows will not allow you to delete the last computer administrator account on your computer. This ensures that one computer administrator account always exists on the computer.

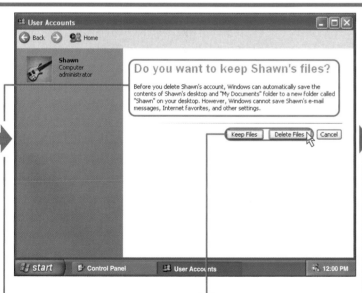

■ Windows asks if you want to keep the user's personal files.

6 Click an option to specify if you want to keep or delete the user's personal files.

■ Windows asks you to confirm that you want to delete the account.

7 Click **Delete Account** to permanently delete the account.

■ Windows deletes the account from your computer.

8 Click ☒ to close the User Accounts window.

You can assign a password to your user account to prevent other people from accessing the account. You will need to enter the password each time you want to use Windows.

You should choose a password that is at least seven characters long and contains a random combination of letters, numbers and symbols. Do not use words that people can easily associate with you, such as your name.

If you have a computer administrator account, you can assign passwords to all accounts. If you have a limited account, you can assign a password only to your own account. For information on the types of accounts, see page 118.

ASSIGN A PASSWORD TO A USER ACCOUNT

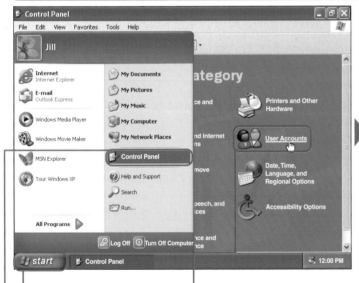

1 Click **start** to display the Start menu.

2 Click **Control Panel** to change your computer's settings.

■ The Control Panel window appears.

3 Click **User Accounts** to work with the user accounts set up on your computer.

■ The User Accounts window appears.

■ If you have a limited account, skip to step 5.

■ If you have a computer administrator account, this area displays the accounts set up on your computer.

4 Click the account you want to assign a password to.

122

When assigning a password to my user account, why does Windows ask if I want to make my files and folders private?

When you assign a password to your user account, other users can still access your files and folders. If you do not want other people to have access to your files and folders, you can make your files and folders private. Click **Yes, Make Private** or **No** to specify if you want to make your files and folders private. For more information on making your files and folders private, see page 128.

> **Do you want to make your files and folders private?**
>
> Even with a password on your account, other people using this computer can still see your documents. To prevent this, Windows can make your files and folders private. This will prevent users with limited accounts from gaining access to your files and folders.
>
> [Yes, Make Private] [No]

How can I change the password I assigned to my user account?

To change your password, perform steps **1** to **5** below, except click **Change my password** in step **5**. Then type your current password and perform steps **6** to **9** below, except click **Change Password** in step **9**.

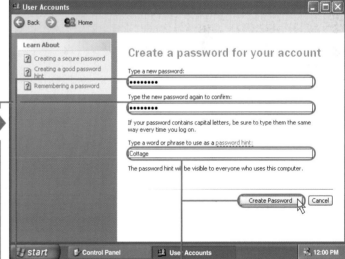

■ A list of tasks that you can perform to change the account appears.

5 Click **Create a password** to assign a password to the account.

6 Click this area and type a password for the account.

7 Click this area and type the password again to confirm the password.

8 Click this area and type a word or phrase that can help you remember the password. This information will be available to everyone who uses the computer.

9 Click **Create Password**.

You can log off Windows so another person can log on to Windows to use the computer.

When you log off Windows, you can choose to keep your programs and files open while another person uses the computer. This allows you to quickly return to your programs and files after the other person finishes using the computer.

LOG OFF WINDOWS

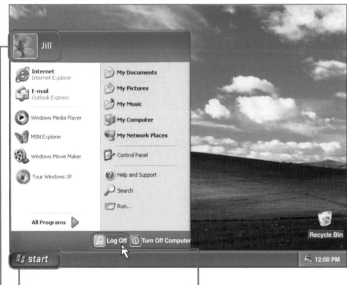

1 Click **start** to display the Start menu.

■ This area displays the name of the current user account.

2 Click **Log Off** to log off Windows.

■ The Log Off Windows dialog box appears.

3 Click one of the following options.

Switch User
Log off Windows, keeping your programs and files open.

Log Off
Log off Windows, closing your open programs and files.

■ The Welcome screen appears, allowing another person to log on to Windows to use the computer. To log on to Windows, see page 125.

LOG ON TO WINDOWS

If you have set up user accounts on your computer, you will need to log on to Windows to use the computer.

You must log on to Windows each time you turn on your computer or log off Windows to switch between user accounts. For information on logging off Windows, see page 124.

LOG ON TO WINDOWS

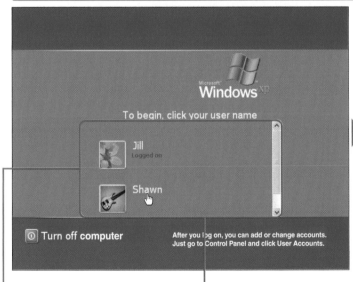

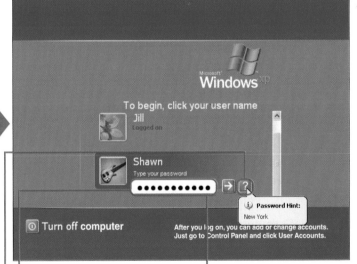

■ When you turn on your computer or log off Windows to switch between user accounts, the Welcome screen appears.

■ This area displays the user accounts set up on your computer.

1 Click the name of your user account.

■ If you assigned a password to your user account, a box appears that allows you to enter your password.

■ If you cannot remember your password, click [?] to display the password hint you entered when you created the password.

2 Click this area and type your password. Then press the [Enter] key to log on to Windows.

■ Windows starts, displaying your own personalized files and computer settings.

125

You can view the personal files of every user set up on your computer.

In most cases, the contents of every user's My Documents folder and its subfolders are available to other users set up on your computer.

If your computer uses the NTFS file system, you cannot view the personal files of other users if you have a limited user account or a user has made their personal folders private. For information on making personal folders private, see page 128.

VIEW SHARED FILES

1 Click **start** to display the Start menu.

2 Click **My Computer** to view the contents of your computer.

■ The My Computer window appears.

■ The Shared Documents folder contains files that users have selected to share with all other users set up on your computer.

■ This area displays a folder for each user set up on your computer. Each folder contains a user's personal files.

3 To display the contents of a folder, double-click the folder.

SHARE FILES

If you want to share files with every user set up on your computer, you can copy the files to the Shared Documents folder.

Copying files to the Shared Documents folder is useful when you want to share files that are not stored in the My Documents folder or if your computer uses the NTFS file system and other users are restricted from viewing the contents of your My Documents folder.

SHARE FILES

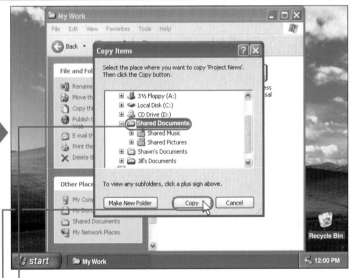

1 Click the file you want to share with every user set up on your computer.

■ To share more than one file, select all the files you want to share. To select multiple files, see page 34.

2 Click **Copy this file**.

*Note: If you selected multiple files, click **Copy the selected items** in step 2.*

■ The Copy Items dialog box appears.

3 Click **Shared Documents**.

4 Click **Copy** to copy the file.

■ Windows places a copy of the file in the Shared Documents folder. The file is now available to every user set up on your computer.

Note: If you no longer want to share a file, delete the file from the Shared Documents folder. To view the contents of the Shared Documents folder, see page 126. To delete a file, see page 44.

MAKE YOUR PERSONAL FOLDERS PRIVATE

You can make the contents of your personal folders private so that only you can access the files within the folders. Your personal folders include the My Documents folder and its subfolders.

You can make your personal folders private only if your computer uses the NTFS file system. The file system is typically determined when you install Windows.

If your computer uses the NTFS file system, the contents of your personal folders are available to every user with an administrator account set up on your computer.

MAKE YOUR PERSONAL FOLDERS PRIVATE

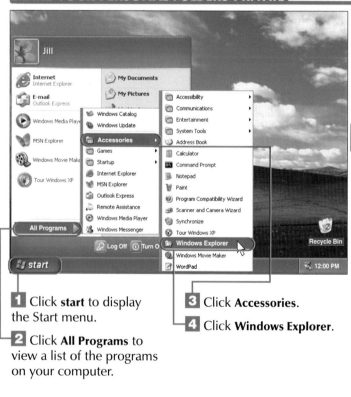

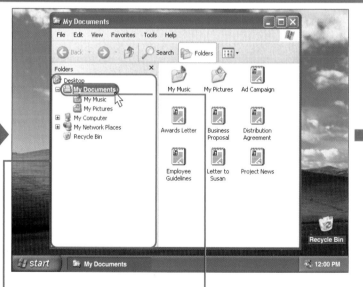

1 Click **start** to display the Start menu.

2 Click **All Programs** to view a list of the programs on your computer.

3 Click **Accessories**.

4 Click **Windows Explorer**.

■ A window appears, allowing you to view the contents of your computer.

■ This area displays the organization of the folders on your computer.

5 Click the **My Documents** folder to specify that you want to make the contents of this folder private.

Note: To make just one subfolder within the My Documents folder private, click the subfolder you want to make private.

What do I need to consider before making my personal folders private?

Before making your personal folders private, you should assign a password to your user account. If you do not assign a password to your user account, anyone will be able to log on to your account and view the contents of your personal folders even if you make the folders private. To assign a password to your user account, see page 122.

After making my personal folders private, can I share just one file in the folders?

Yes. To share a specific file with every user set up on your computer, you need to place a copy of the file in the Shared Documents folder. The Shared Documents folder contains files that every user set up on your computer can access. For information on the Shared Documents folder, see page 127.

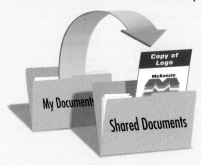

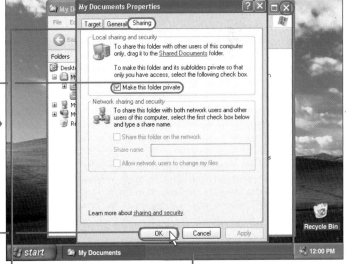

6 Click **File**.

7 Click **Properties**.

■ The My Documents Properties dialog box appears.

8 Click the **Sharing** tab.

9 Click **Make this folder private** to make the My Documents folder and all its files and subfolders private (☐ changes to ☑).

10 Click **OK** to confirm your change.

11 Click ☒ to close the Windows Explorer window.

■ If you no longer want to make your personal folders private, perform steps **1** to **11** (☑ changes to ☐ in step **9**).

CHAPTER 7

CUSTOMIZE AND OPTIMIZE WINDOWS

Windows XP includes several features that allow you to customize and optimize your computer. In this chapter, you will learn how to change the screen saver, install programs, obtain the latest Windows XP updates and more.

You can select a picture, background color or both to decorate your desktop.

When selecting a picture to decorate your desktop, you can use a picture that Windows provides or your own picture.

CHANGE THE DESKTOP BACKGROUND

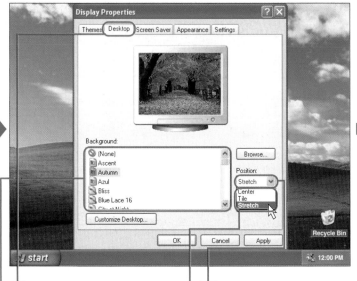

1 Right-click a blank area on your desktop. A menu appears.

2 Click **Properties**.

■ The Display Properties dialog box appears.

3 Click the **Desktop** tab.

4 To display a picture on your desktop, click the picture you want to use.

Note: Pictures stored in your My Pictures folder appear in the list.

5 To select how you want to display the picture on your desktop, click this area.

6 Click the way you want to display the picture.

How can I display a picture on my desktop?

Windows offers three ways that you can display a picture on your desktop.

Center

Displays the picture in the middle of your desktop.

Tile

Repeats the picture until it fills your entire desktop.

Stretch

Stretches the picture to cover your entire desktop.

Note: If you select a large picture that fills your entire desktop, selecting one of these options will have no effect on the way the picture will appear on your desktop.

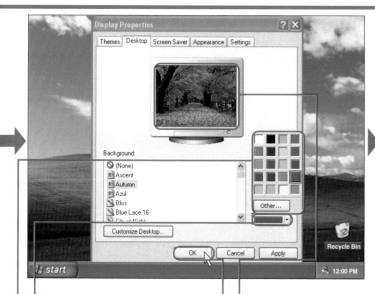 

7 To select a color for your desktop, click this area to display a list of the available colors.

8 Click the color you want to use.

Note: If you selected a picture in step 4, the color you select will fill any space not covered by the picture.

■ This area displays how the picture and/or color will appear on your desktop.

9 Click **OK** to add the picture and/or color to your desktop.

■ The picture and/or color appear on your desktop.

■ To remove a picture from your desktop, perform steps 1 to 4, selecting (**None**) in step 4. Then perform step 9.

You can change the style and colors that Windows uses to display windows and other items on your screen.

CHANGE THE SCREEN APPEARANCE

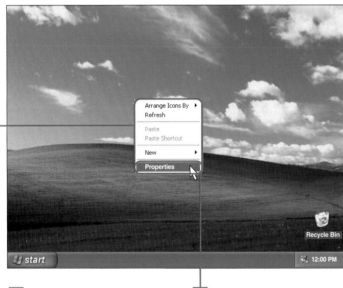

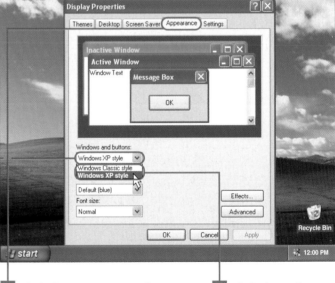

1 Right-click a blank area on your desktop. A menu appears.

2 Click **Properties**.

■ The Display Properties dialog box appears.

3 Click the **Appearance** tab.

4 Click this area to display the available styles.

5 Click the style you want to use.

SIMPLIFY IT

How can I change the appearance of my screen?

Windows XP style

Windows Classic style

Windows and buttons

By default, you can choose between the Windows XP style, which is the default style of Windows XP, and the Windows Classic style, which is the style used in previous versions of Windows.

Color scheme

You can change the colors used in items such as windows, dialog boxes and the Start menu.

Font size

You can change the size of text shown in items such as menus, icons and the title bars of windows. Changing the font size will also change the size of some buttons, such as the Close button (☒). Increasing the font size is useful if you have trouble reading the text on your screen or clicking small buttons.

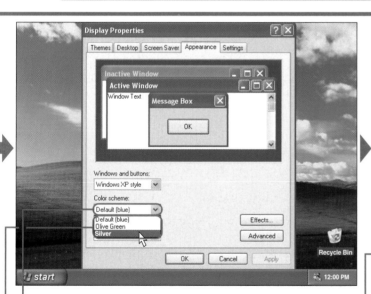

6 Click this area to display the available color schemes.

7 Click the color scheme you want to use.

Note: The available color schemes depend on the style you selected in step 5.

8 Click this area to display the available font sizes.

9 Click the font size you want to use.

Note: The available font sizes depend on the color scheme you selected in step 7.

■ This area displays a preview of how your screen will appear.

10 Click **OK** to change the appearance of your screen.

A screen saver is a moving picture or pattern that appears on the screen when you do not use your computer for a period of time.

You can use a screen saver to hide your work while you are away from your desk.

By default, Windows will display a screen saver when you do not use your computer for ten minutes.

CHANGE THE SCREEN SAVER

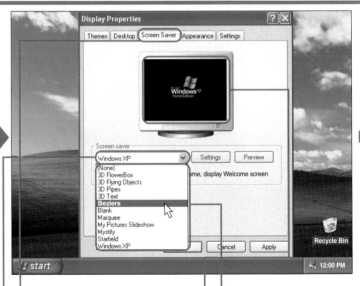

1 Right-click a blank area on your desktop. A menu appears.

2 Click **Properties**.

■ The Display Properties dialog box appears.

3 Click the **Screen Saver** tab.

4 Click this area to display a list of the available screen savers.

5 Click the screen saver you want to use.

■ This area will display a preview of how the screen saver will appear on your screen.

136

Do I need to use a screen saver?

Screen savers were originally designed to prevent screen burn, which occurs when an image appears in a fixed position on the screen for a period of time. Today's monitors are less susceptible to screen burn, but people still use screen savers for their entertainment value.

What does the My Pictures Slideshow screen saver do?

You can select the My Pictures Slideshow screen saver to have the pictures stored in your My Pictures folder appear as your screen saver. Windows will rotate through all the pictures in the folder, displaying each picture on your screen for six seconds at a time. To view the contents of your My Pictures folder, see page 23.

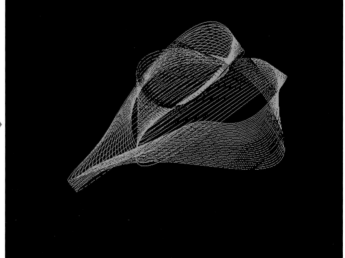

6 To specify the number of minutes your computer must be inactive before the screen saver will appear, double-click this area. Then type the number of minutes.

7 If multiple users are set up on your computer, this option requires you to log on to Windows each time you remove the screen saver. You can click this option to turn the option off (☑ changes to ☐).

Note: For information on logging on to Windows, see page 125.

8 Click **OK**.

■ The screen saver appears when you do not use your computer for the number of minutes you specified.

■ You can move the mouse or press a key on the keyboard to remove the screen saver from your screen.

■ To stop a screen saver from appearing, perform steps **1** to **5**, selecting (**None**) in step **5**. Then perform step **8**.

You should make sure the correct date and time are set in your computer. Windows uses the date and time to determine when you create and update your files.

Your computer has a built-in clock that keeps track of the date and time even when you turn off your computer.

CHANGE THE DATE AND TIME

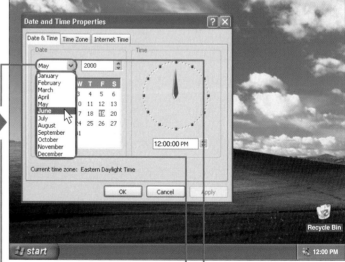

■ This area displays the time set in your computer.

1 To display the date set in your computer, position the mouse ⟋ over the time. After a moment, the date appears.

2 To change the date or time set in your computer, double-click this area.

■ The Date and Time Properties dialog box appears.

■ This area displays the month set in your computer.

3 To change the month, click this area.

4 Click the correct month.

138

Will Windows ever change the time automatically?

Windows will change the time automatically to compensate for daylight saving time. When you turn on your computer after daylight saving time occurs, Windows will have automatically changed the time.

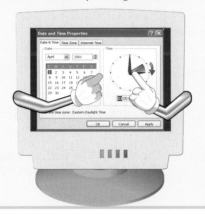

Can Windows ensure that my computer's clock is accurate?

Windows automatically synchronizes your computer's clock with a time server on the Internet approximately once a week. You must be connected to the Internet for the synchronization to occur. If you are on a network that uses a firewall to protect against unauthorized access, Windows will not be able to synchronize your computer's clock.

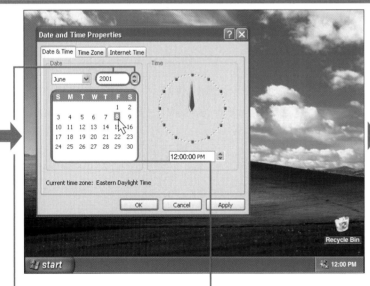

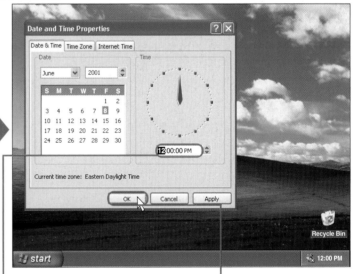

■ This area displays the year set in your computer.

5 To change the year, click ▲ or ▼ in this area until the correct year appears.

■ This area displays the days in the month. The current day is highlighted.

6 To change the day, click the correct day.

■ This area displays the time set in your computer.

7 To change the time, double-click the part of the time you want to change. Then type the correct information.

8 Click **OK** to confirm your changes.

Windows can play sound effects when certain program events occur on your computer. For example, you can hear a short tune when you start Windows.

You can change the sounds assigned to many events at once by selecting a sound scheme. A sound scheme consists of a set of related sounds.

ASSIGN SOUNDS TO PROGRAM EVENTS

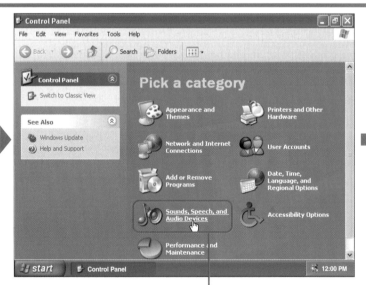

1 Click **start** to display the Start menu.

2 Click **Control Panel** to change your computer's settings.

■ The Control Panel window appears.

3 Click **Sounds, Speech, and Audio Devices**.

What program events can Windows assign sounds to?

Windows can assign sounds to over 30 events on your computer. Here are some examples.

Exit Windows

A sound will play each time you exit Windows.

tjones@abc.com

New Mail Notification

A sound will play each time you receive a new e-mail message.

Empty Recycle Bin

A sound will play each time you empty the Recycle Bin.

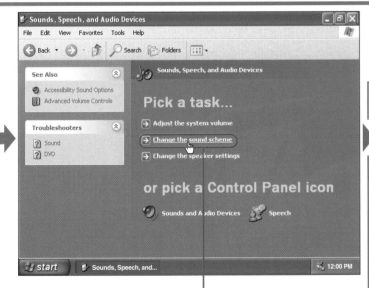

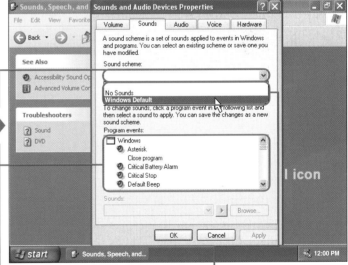

■ The Sounds, Speech, and Audio Devices window appears.

4 Click **Change the sound scheme** to assign sounds to program events on your computer.

■ The Sounds and Audio Devices Properties dialog box appears.

■ This area lists the events that you can assign sounds to.

5 Click this area to display a list of the available sound schemes.

6 Click the sound scheme you want to use.

*Note: If you do not want sounds to play for any events, select **No Sounds**.*

CONTINUED

When assigning sounds to program events, you can test the sound that Windows will play for each event.

ASSIGN SOUNDS TO PROGRAM EVENTS (CONTINUED)

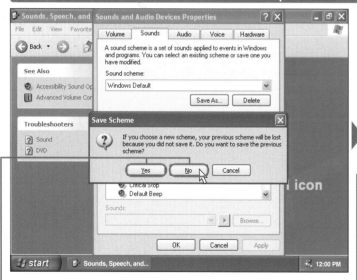

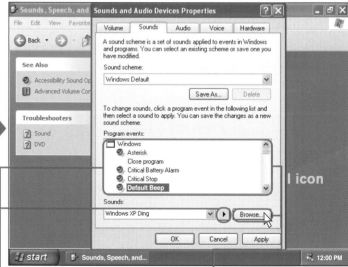

■ The Save Scheme dialog box may appear, asking if you want to save the previous sound scheme.

7 Click **Yes** or **No** to specify if you want to save the previous sound scheme.

*Note: If you selected **Yes**, a dialog box will appear, allowing you to name the sound scheme. Type a name for the sound scheme and then press the* **Enter** *key. The sound scheme will appear in the list of available sound schemes.*

■ A speaker icon (🔊) appears beside each event that will play a sound.

8 To play the sound for an event, click the event.

9 Click ▶ to play the sound.

ASSIGN SOUNDS TO SPECIFIC EVENTS

10 To assign a sound to a specific event, click the event.

11 Click **Browse** to search for the sound you want to use.

SIMPLIFY IT

Where can I obtain sounds that I can assign to specific program events?

You can use the sounds included with Windows, purchase collections of sounds at computer stores or obtain sounds on the Internet. The sounds you use must be in the Wave format. Wave files have the .wav extension, such as chimes.wav. You can obtain sounds at the following Web sites.

www.favewavs.com

www.wavlist.com

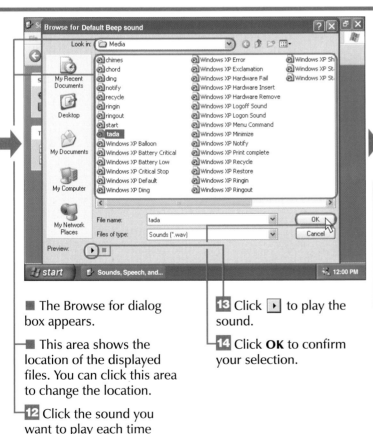

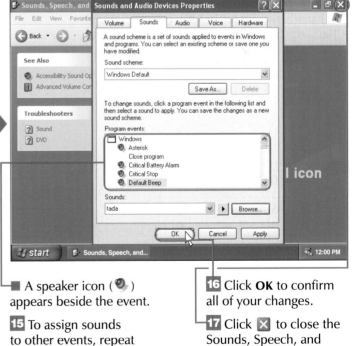

■ The Browse for dialog box appears.

■ This area shows the location of the displayed files. You can click this area to change the location.

12 Click the sound you want to play each time the event occurs.

13 Click ▶ to play the sound.

14 Click **OK** to confirm your selection.

■ A speaker icon (🔊) appears beside the event.

15 To assign sounds to other events, repeat steps **10** to **14** for each event.

16 Click **OK** to confirm all of your changes.

17 Click ✕ to close the Sounds, Speech, and Audio Devices window.

ADJUST THE VOLUME

You can adjust the volume of sound on your computer.

Volume Control

You can adjust the volume of all the devices on your computer at once. You can also adjust the volume of specific devices without affecting the volume of other devices.

ADJUST THE VOLUME

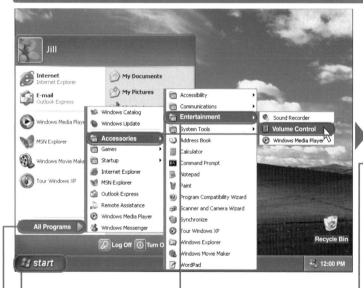

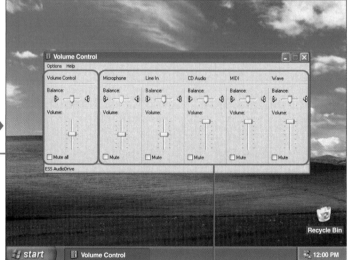

1 Click **start** to display the Start menu.

2 Click **All Programs** to view a list of the programs on your computer.

3 Click **Accessories**.

4 Click **Entertainment**.

5 Click **Volume Control**.

■ A window appears that allows you to change the sound volume on your computer.

■ This area displays the control that allows you to change the volume of all the devices on your computer at once.

■ This area displays controls that allow you to change the volume of individual devices on your computer.

Note: The available devices depend on the sound capabilities of your computer.

Is there a quick way to adjust the speaker volume?

Many speakers have a volume dial that you can use to adjust the volume. Your speakers may also have a power button that you can use to turn the sound on or off.

What devices can I adjust the volume for?

Windows allows you to adjust the volume of many devices on your computer. Here are some common devices for which you can adjust the volume.

Device	Controls
Microphone	Recording volume when using a microphone to record sounds.
Line In	Recording volume of devices, such as a CD player or tape player, that connect to the Line In port. The Line In port is usually located at the back of a computer.
CD Audio	Playback volume of audio CDs.
MIDI	Playback volume of MIDI sounds.
Wave	Playback volume of Wave sounds.

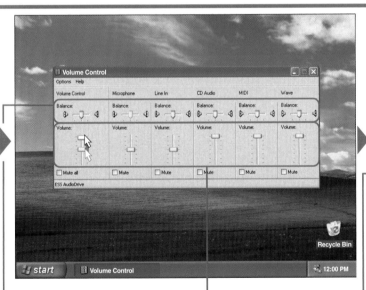

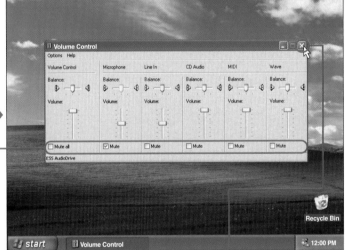

6 To change the balance between the left and right speakers for a device, drag the balance slider ( ) for the device.

Note: Changing the balance between the left and right speakers is useful when one speaker is farther away than the other and you want to make that speaker louder.

7 To increase or decrease the volume for a device, drag the volume slider ( ) for the device.

8 To turn off the sound for a device, click **Mute** for the device (changes to).

Note: To once again turn on the sound for a device, repeat step 8.

9 When you finish adjusting the volume, click to close the window.

INSTALL A PROGRAM

You can install a new program on your computer. Programs are available on CD-ROM discs and floppy disks.

After you install a new program, make sure you keep the program's CD-ROM disc or floppy disks in a safe place. If your computer fails or you accidentally erase the program's files, you may need to install the program again.

You can only use the method below to install programs designed for Windows.

INSTALL A PROGRAM

■ Before installing a program, you should close all open programs.

1 Click **start** to display the Start menu.

2 Click **Control Panel** to change your computer's settings.

■ The Control Panel window appears.

3 Click **Add or Remove Programs**.

■ The Add or Remove Programs window appears.

4 Click **Add New Programs** to install a new program.

5 To install a program from a CD-ROM disc or floppy disk, click **CD or Floppy**.

Why did an installation program appear when I inserted a program's CD-ROM disc into my CD-ROM drive?

Most Windows programs available on a CD-ROM disc will automatically start an installation program when you insert the disc into your CD-ROM drive. Follow the instructions on your screen to install the program.

How can I install a program I obtained on the Internet?

You can obtain many useful programs on the Internet, such as at the www.shareware.com Web site. To install a program you obtained on the Internet, locate the program's files on your computer and then double-click the file that allows you to install the program. The file is usually named **install**, **setup** or the name of the program.

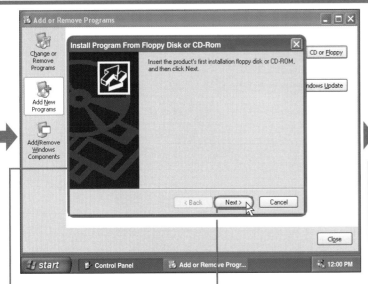

■ The Install Program From Floppy Disk or CD-ROM dialog box appears.

6 Insert the program's first installation floppy disk or CD-ROM disc into the appropriate drive on your computer.

7 Click **Next** to continue.

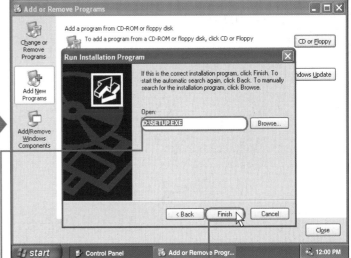

■ The Run Installation Program dialog box appears.

■ This area displays the location and name of the installation program that Windows will run to install the program.

8 Click **Finish** to install the program.

9 Follow the instructions on your screen. Every program will ask you a different set of questions.

You can remove a program you no longer use from your computer. Removing a program will free up space on your computer.

REMOVE A PROGRAM

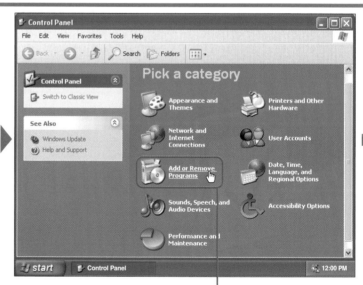

1 Click **start** to display the Start menu.

2 Click **Control Panel** to change your computer's settings.

■ The Control Panel window appears.

3 Click **Add or Remove Programs**.

Why doesn't the program I want to remove appear in the Add or Remove Programs window?

You can only use the Add or Remove Programs window to remove programs designed for Windows. For all other programs, you can check the documentation supplied with the program to determine how to remove the program from your computer. You can also purchase an uninstall program, such as Norton CleanSweep, that will help you delete unwanted programs from your computer.

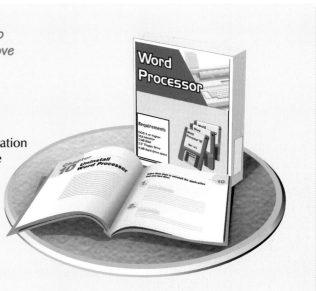

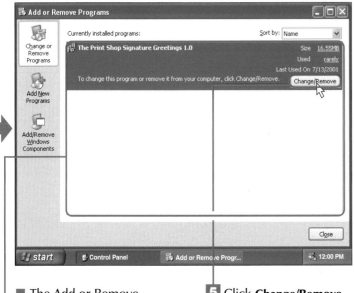

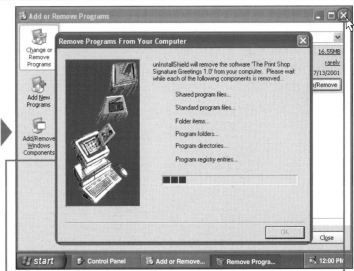

■ The Add or Remove Programs window appears.

■ This area lists the programs installed on your computer.

4 Click the name of the program you want to remove.

5 Click **Change/Remove** or **Remove**.

Note: The name of the button depends on the program you are removing.

■ Windows begins the process of removing the program from your computer.

6 Follow the instructions on your screen. Every program will take you through different steps to remove the program.

7 When Windows has successfully removed the program, click ☒ to close the Add or Remove Programs window.

149

You can set up Windows to automatically keep your computer up to date with the latest Windows updates available on the Internet.

You need an Internet connection for Windows to be able to update your computer automatically.

UPDATE WINDOWS

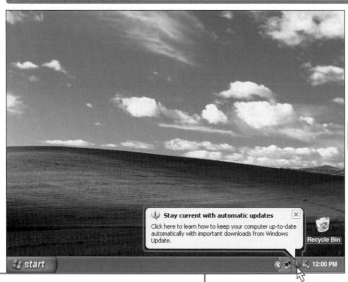

SET UP AUTOMATIC UPDATES

■ An icon (🛡) and message appear when you can set up Windows to update your computer automatically.

1 Click the icon (🛡) to set up Windows to update your computer automatically.

Note: If 🛡 is hidden, you can click 🔇 on the taskbar to display the icon.

■ The Automatic Updates Setup Wizard appears, allowing you to set up Windows to update your computer automatically.

■ This area displays information about updating your computer automatically.

2 Click **Next** to continue.

How will Windows update my computer?

Windows will use the latest information available on the Internet to check for outdated Windows software on your computer. To improve the performance of your computer, Windows can update existing software, fix software problems and add new software. Windows can also obtain updated help information and drivers. A driver is software that enables your computer to communicate with a hardware device, such as a printer.

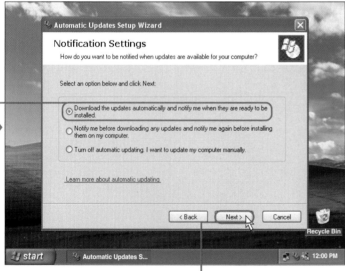

■ Windows asks how you want to be notified when updates are available for your computer.

3 Click this option to have Windows download the updates to your computer automatically and notify you when they are ready to be installed (○ changes to ◉).

4 Click **Next** to continue.

■ This message appears when you have successfully completed the wizard.

5 Click **Finish** to close the wizard.

■ Windows is now set up to update your computer automatically. When you are connected to the Internet, Windows will notify you when updates are available for your computer.

CONTINUED

INSTALL UPDATES

■ When you are connected to the Internet, an icon (🔄) and message appear when updates have been downloaded and are ready to be installed on your computer.

1 Click the icon (🔄) to install the recommended updates.

Note: If 🔄 is hidden, you can click ◀ on the taskbar to display the icon.

■ The Automatic Updates wizard appears, stating that Windows is ready to install the recommended updates for your computer.

■ This area indicates that some updates require you to restart your computer. Before continuing, make sure you save your work and close any open programs.

2 Click **Install** to install the updates.

Is there another way that I can update Windows?

You can install specific updates from the Windows Update Web site. The Windows Update Web site can scan your computer to determine which updates you can install to update Windows. To display the Windows Update Web site, perform the following steps.

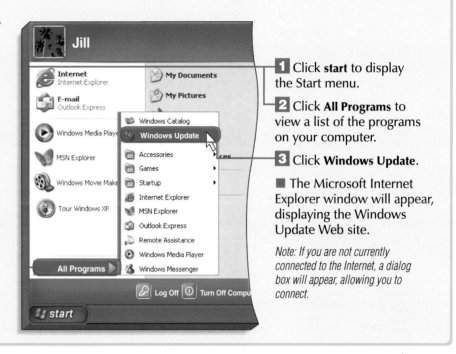

1 Click **start** to display the Start menu.

2 Click **All Programs** to view a list of the programs on your computer.

3 Click **Windows Update**.

■ The Microsoft Internet Explorer window will appear, displaying the Windows Update Web site.

Note: If you are not currently connected to the Internet, a dialog box will appear, allowing you to connect.

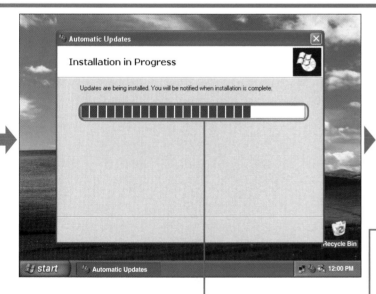

■ Windows installs the updates on your computer.

■ This area shows the progress of the installation.

■ This message appears if you need to restart your computer to complete the installation.

3 Click **Yes** to restart your computer and complete the installation.

*Note: If the "Installation Complete" message appears, you do not need to restart your computer. Click **OK** to complete the installation.*

INSTALL A PRINTER

Before you can use a printer attached to your computer, you need to install the printer on your computer. You need to install a printer only once.

Windows provides a wizard that guides you step by step through the process of installing a printer.

Before installing a printer, make sure you connect the printer to your computer and turn on the printer.

INSTALL A PRINTER

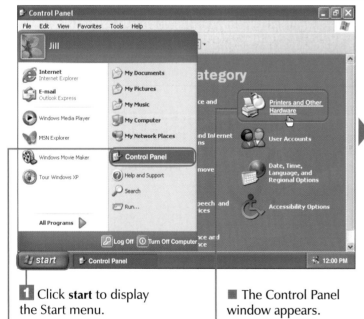

1 Click **start** to display the Start menu.

2 Click **Control Panel** to change your computer's settings.

■ The Control Panel window appears.

3 Click **Printers and Other Hardware**.

■ The Printers and Other Hardware window appears.

4 Click **View installed printers or fax printers**.

Why do I need to install a printer?

Installing a printer allows you to install the printer driver that Windows needs to work with the printer. A printer driver is special software that enables Windows to communicate with a printer.

How do I install a Plug and Play printer?

A Plug and Play printer is a printer that Windows can automatically detect and install. Most new printers are Plug and Play. The first time you connect a Plug and Play printer to your computer and turn on the printer, Windows will usually install the printer without requiring you to make any selections. In some cases, the Found New Hardware Wizard appears, displaying instructions you can follow to install the printer.

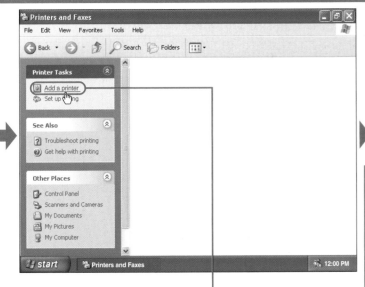

■ The Printers and Faxes window appears.

5 Click **Add a printer** to install a new printer.

■ The Add Printer Wizard appears.

■ This area describes how you can install a Plug and Play printer without using the wizard. For more information on installing a Plug and Play printer, see the top of this page.

6 Click **Next** to continue.

CONTINUED

INSTALL A PRINTER

When installing a printer, you need to specify which port you want the printer to use. A port is a socket where you plug a device into a computer.

Ports are usually located at the back of a computer and allow a computer to communicate with the connected devices.

INSTALL A PRINTER (CONTINUED)

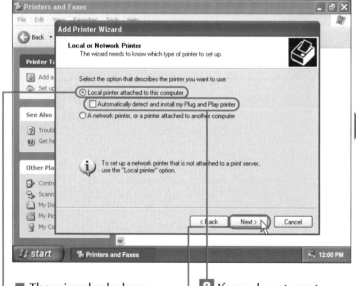

■ The wizard asks how the printer connects to your computer.

7 Click this option to install a printer that connects directly to your computer (○ changes to ⦿).

8 If you do not want Windows to automatically detect and install a Plug and Play printer connected to your computer, click this option (☑ changes to ☐).

9 Click **Next** to continue.

10 This area displays the port your printer will use to communicate with your computer. You can click this area to select a different port.

Note: Most printers use the LPT1 port.

11 Click **Next** to continue.

156

What should I do if the printer I want to install does not appear in the list?

If the printer you want to install does not appear in the list of printers in step **13** below, you can use the installation disk that came with your printer.

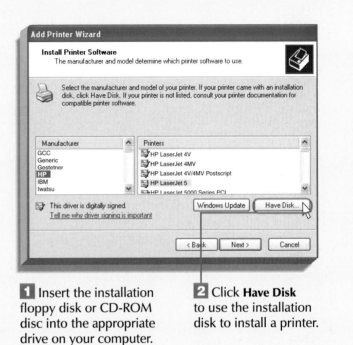

1 Insert the installation floppy disk or CD-ROM disc into the appropriate drive on your computer.

2 Click **Have Disk** to use the installation disk to install a printer.

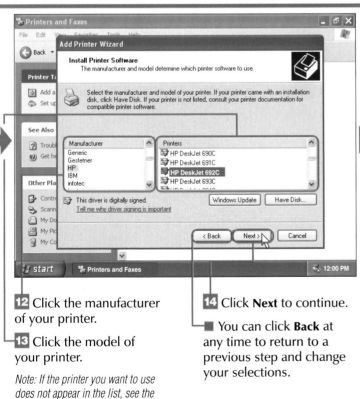

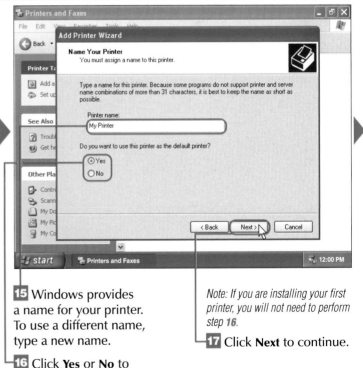

12 Click the manufacturer of your printer.

13 Click the model of your printer.

Note: If the printer you want to use does not appear in the list, see the top of this page.

14 Click **Next** to continue.

■ You can click **Back** at any time to return to a previous step and change your selections.

15 Windows provides a name for your printer. To use a different name, type a new name.

16 Click **Yes** or **No** to specify if you want to use the printer as your default printer ($\bigcirc$ changes to $\odot$). Files will automatically print to the default printer.

*Note: If you are installing your first printer, you will not need to perform step **16**.*

17 Click **Next** to continue.

CONTINUED

157

INSTALL A PRINTER

> If your computer is set up on a network, you can share your printer with other people on the network. Sharing a printer allows other people to use your printer to print documents.

Sharing a printer allows individuals and companies to save money since several people on a network can use the same printer.

INSTALL A PRINTER (CONTINUED)

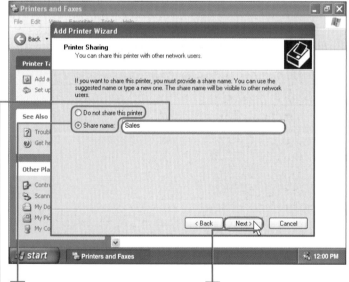

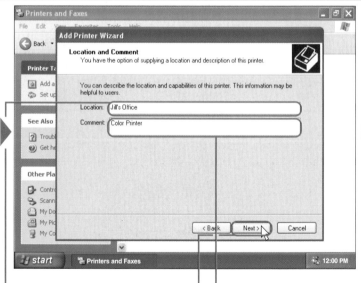

18 Click an option to specify if you want to share the printer on your network (○ changes to ◉).

19 If you selected to share the printer, this area displays the printer name people will see on the network. To use a different printer name, type a new name.

20 Click **Next** to continue.

■ If you chose not to share your printer in step **18**, skip to step **24**.

■ Windows allows you to enter information about your printer that can be helpful to other people on your network.

21 Click this area and type the location of your printer.

22 Click this area and type a comment about your printer, such as its capabilities.

23 Click **Next** to continue.

How can I view the printer I installed on my computer?

The Printers and Faxes window displays an icon for the printer you installed on your computer. If you chose to share your printer with other people on your network, a hand (☝) appears in the icon for the shared printer. The Printers and Faxes window may also display an icon for each printer on your network that is available for you to use. To view the Printers and Faxes window, perform steps 1 to 4 on page 154.

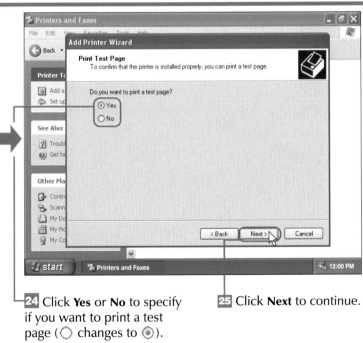

24 Click **Yes** or **No** to specify if you want to print a test page (○ changes to ●).

Note: A test page will confirm that your printer is installed properly. If you choose to print a test page, make sure your printer is turned on.

25 Click **Next** to continue.

■ This area indicates that you have successfully completed the wizard.

■ This area displays the settings you selected for your printer.

26 Click **Finish** to install the printer.

Note: If you chose to print a test page in step 24, a dialog box will appear, confirming that the test page printed correctly. Click OK if the test page printed correctly.

If you are experiencing problems with your computer, you can use the System Restore feature to return your computer to a time before the problems occurred.

For example, if your computer does not work properly after you install a program, you can restore your computer to a time before you installed the program.

RESTORE YOUR COMPUTER

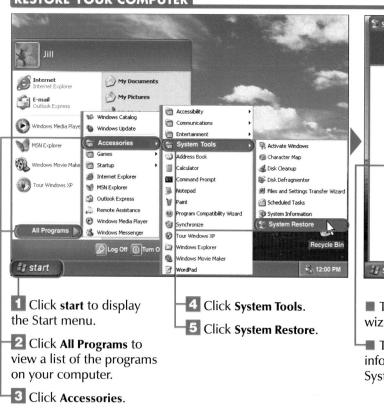

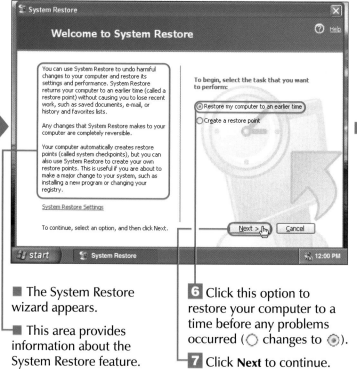

1 Click **start** to display the Start menu.

2 Click **All Programs** to view a list of the programs on your computer.

3 Click **Accessories**.

4 Click **System Tools**.

5 Click **System Restore**.

■ The System Restore wizard appears.

■ This area provides information about the System Restore feature.

6 Click this option to restore your computer to a time before any problems occurred (○ changes to ◉).

7 Click **Next** to continue.

What types of restore points are available?

When restoring your computer, you can select from several types of restore points. A restore point is an earlier, more stable time that you can return your computer to.

Windows can store between one to three weeks of restore points. Here are a few common types of restore points.

System Checkpoint

Restore points created automatically by Windows on a regular basis.

Installed (*Program*)

Restore points created automatically when you install certain programs. The name of the program appears beside the word "Installed."

Automatic Updates Install

Restore points created when you install the recommended updates for Windows. For information on automatically updating Windows, see page 150.

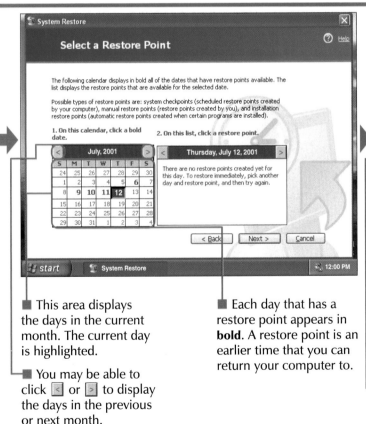

■ This area displays the days in the current month. The current day is highlighted.

■ You may be able to click < or > to display the days in the previous or next month.

■ Each day that has a restore point appears in **bold**. A restore point is an earlier time that you can return your computer to.

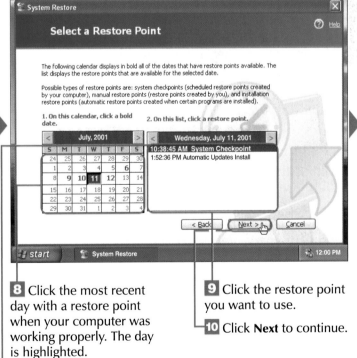

8 Click the most recent day with a restore point when your computer was working properly. The day is highlighted.

■ This area lists the restore points available for the day you selected.

9 Click the restore point you want to use.

10 Click **Next** to continue.

CONTINUED

When you restore your computer to an earlier time, you will not lose any of your recent work, such as documents or e-mail messages.

Before restoring your computer to an earlier time, you should close all open files and programs.

RESTORE YOUR COMPUTER (CONTINUED)

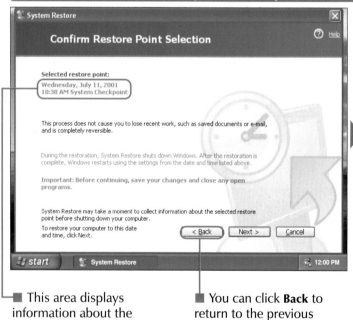

■ This area displays information about the restore point you selected.

■ You can click **Back** to return to the previous screen and change the restore point you selected.

■ This area displays information about the System Restore feature.

11 Click **Next** to restore your computer.

Will I need to re-install any programs after restoring my computer?

When you restore your computer to an earlier time, any programs you installed after that date may be uninstalled. Files you created using the program will not be deleted, but you will need to re-install the program to work with the files again.

Can I reverse the changes made when I restored my computer?

Yes. Any changes that the System Restore feature makes to your computer are completely reversible. To undo your last restoration, perform steps **1** to **7** on page 160, except select **Undo my last restoration** in step **6**. Then perform steps **11** and **12** below.

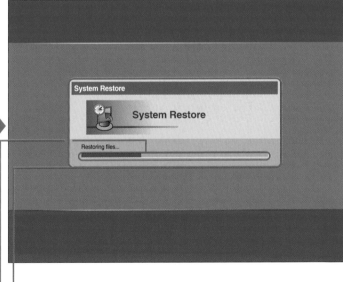

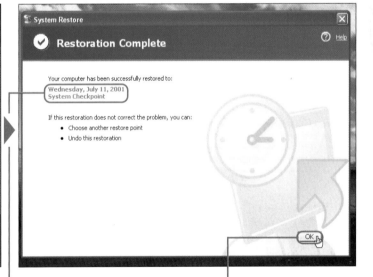

■ The System Restore dialog box appears.

■ This area shows the progress of the restoration.

■ When the restoration is complete, your computer will automatically restart.

■ After your computer restarts, a dialog box appears, indicating that your computer has been successfully restored.

■ This area displays the date to which your computer was restored.

12 Click **OK** to close the dialog box.

You can allow a person at another computer to view your computer screen and chat with you to help you solve a computer problem.

With your permission, the other person can control your computer to fix the problem.

If either computer is connected to a network, a firewall may prevent you from using Remote Assistance. A firewall protects a network from unauthorized access.

GET REMOTE ASSISTANCE

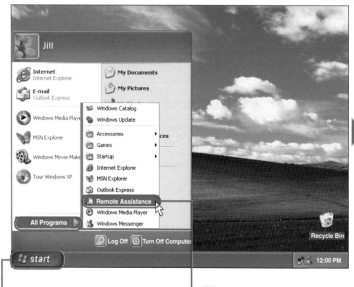

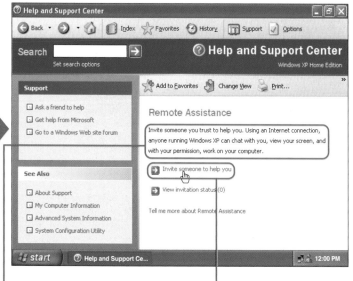

■ You must be connected to the Internet to get remote assistance.

1 Click **start** to display the Start menu.

2 Click **All Programs** to view a list of the programs on your computer.

3 Click **Remote Assistance**.

■ The Help and Support Center window appears.

■ This area displays information about Remote Assistance.

4 Click **Invite someone to help you**.

SIMPLIFY IT

How can I send an invitation for Remote Assistance to another person?

You can send a Remote Assistance invitation to another person in an e-mail message or by using Windows Messenger.

To use Remote Assistance, both computers must use Windows XP and be connected to the Internet.

E-mail

To send an invitation for Remote Assistance in an e-mail message, both computers must use a compatible e-mail program, such as Outlook Express. For information on Outlook Express, see pages 202 to 213.

Windows Messenger

To send an invitation for Remote Assistance using Windows Messenger, both computers must be signed in to Windows Messenger. The person you want to send an invitation to must also appear in your contact list in Windows Messenger. For information on Windows Messenger, see pages 216 to 223.

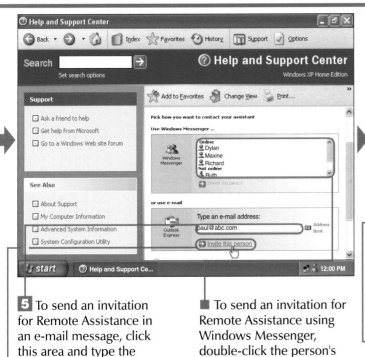

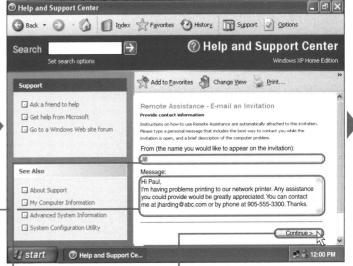

5 To send an invitation for Remote Assistance in an e-mail message, click this area and type the person's e-mail address.

6 Click **Invite this person**.

■ To send an invitation for Remote Assistance using Windows Messenger, double-click the person's name in this area. Then skip to step 14.

7 Double-click this area and type your name.

8 Click this area and type the message you want to include with the invitation.

Note: Your message should include a brief description of your computer problem and indicate how the other person can contact you. Instructions on how to use Remote Assistance are automatically included with the invitation.

9 Click **Continue**.

CONTINUED ▶

GET REMOTE ASSISTANCE

> When sending a Remote Assistance invitation in an e-mail message, you can specify when you want the invitation to expire and a password the other person must enter to connect to your computer.

Specifying an expiration time and password for an invitation protects your computer from unauthorized access.

When specifying a password, do not use your name, user name or a common word. Make sure the password contains at least seven characters and contains letters, numbers and symbols. You must tell the other person the password you specified.

GET REMOTE ASSISTANCE (CONTINUED)

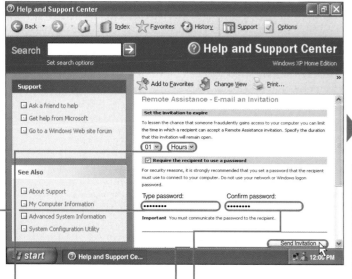

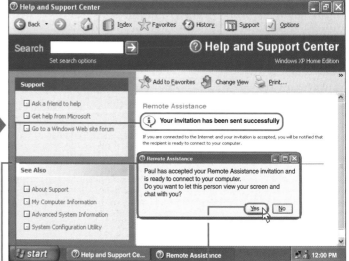

10 These areas indicate when the invitation will expire. You can click an area to change the time.

11 Click this area and type a password the other person must enter to connect to your computer.

12 Click this area and type the password again.

13 Click **Send Invitation**.

■ A dialog box will appear, allowing you to confirm that you want to send the message. Click **Send** to send the message.

■ This message appears when your invitation has been sent successfully.

■ A dialog box appears when the other person accepts your Remote Assistance invitation.

14 Click **Yes** to allow the other person to view your screen and chat with you.

What will the other person's computer screen display?

Once you allow the other person to view your computer screen and chat with you, the Remote Assistance window appears on the person's screen.

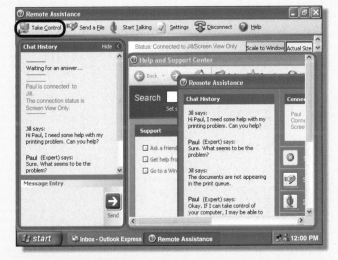

Chat

This area displays the ongoing conversation and an area that allows the other person to send you a message.

Your Computer Screen

This area displays your computer screen. The screen shows the tasks that you or the other person perform.

Take Control

The other person can click **Take Control** to ask your permission to control your computer.

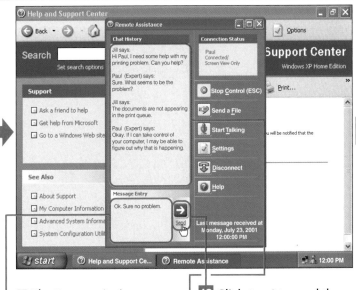

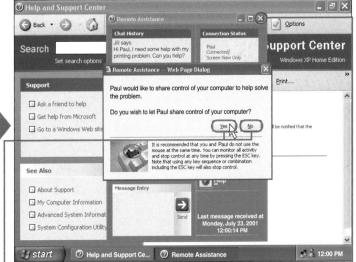

■ The Remote Assistance window appears.

15 To send a message to the other person, click this area and type a message.

16 Click **Send** to send the message.

Note: You can also press the **Enter** *key to send the message.*

■ This area will display the message you sent and the ongoing conversation.

■ A dialog box appears if the other person wants to control your computer.

17 Click **Yes** or **No** to specify if you want the other person to control your computer.

■ To stop the other person from controlling your computer, press the **Esc** key.

*Note: A message appears, indicating that the other person is no longer controlling your computer. Click **OK**.*

18 When you finish using Remote Assistance, click **☒** to close the window.

CHAPTER 8

WORK ON A NETWORK

A network is a group of connected computers. This chapter teaches you how to share information and printers on a network, as well as set up your own home network.

BROWSE THROUGH A NETWORK

You can use My Network Places to browse through the information available on your network.

You can work with the files available on your network as you would work with files stored on your own computer.

BROWSE THROUGH A NETWORK

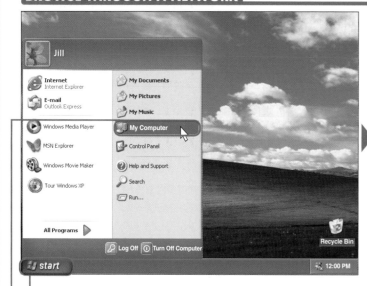

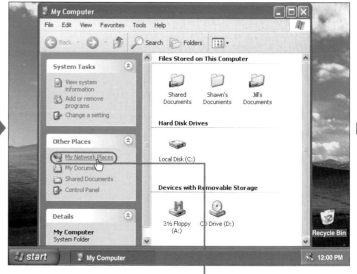

1 Click **start** to display the Start menu.

2 Click **My Computer** to view the contents of your computer.

■ If My Network Places appears on the Start menu, click **My Network Places** and then skip to step **4**.

■ The My Computer window appears.

3 Click **My Network Places** to browse through the information available on your network.

Why can I no longer access a folder on my network?

You will not be able to access a folder on your network if the computer that stores the folder is turned off or if the owner of the computer stops sharing the folder.

Can two people on a network work on the same file at once?

Most programs, such as word processors, allow only one person to make changes to a file at one time. Some programs, such as database programs, may allow several people on a network to make changes to a file at the same time.

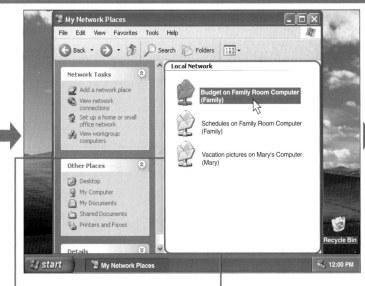

■ The My Network Places window appears.

■ This area displays all the shared folders available on your network.

4 To display the contents of a folder, double-click the folder.

■ The contents of the folder appear.

■ To open a file, double-click the file.

■ You can click **Back** to return to the previous window.

5 When you finish working with files on your network, click ☒ to close the window.

171

SHARE INFORMATION

You can specify the information on your computer that you want to share with other people on your network.

Sharing information is useful when people on a network need to access the same files.

SHARE INFORMATION

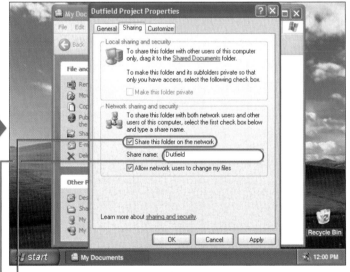

1 Click the folder you want to share with other people on your network.

2 Click **Share this folder**.

■ A Properties dialog box appears.

3 Click this option to share the folder with other people on your network (☐ changes to ☑).

4 This area displays the name of the folder people will see on your network. To change the folder name, drag the mouse I over the current name and then type a new name.

Note: Changing the name of the folder will not change the name of the folder on your computer.

What must I consider before sharing information on my computer?

Before you can share information on your computer with other people on your network, your computer must be set up on the network. To set up your computer on a network, see page 176.

When you set up your computer on a network, Windows automatically shares your Shared Documents folder. For information on the Shared Documents folder, see page 126.

How can I share a folder located on my desktop?

1 To share a folder located on your desktop, right-click the folder. A menu appears.

2 Click **Sharing and Security**. Then perform steps **3** to **6** below to share the folder.

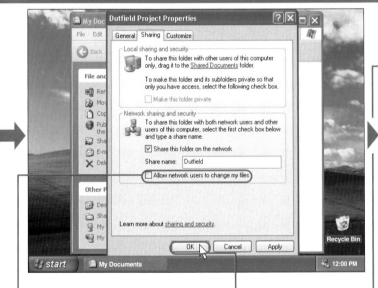

5 If you do not want people on your network to make changes to files in the folder, click this option (☑ changes to ☐).

6 Click **OK** to share the folder.

■ A hand (👆) appears in the icon for the shared folder.

■ Everyone on your network will be able to access all the files within the shared folder.

■ To stop sharing a folder, perform steps **1** to **3** (☑ changes to ☐ in step **3**). Then perform step **6**.

SHARE A PRINTER

You can share your printer with other people on a network. Sharing a printer allows others to use your printer to print documents.

Sharing a printer allows individuals and companies to save money since several people on a network can use the same printer.

To share a printer on a network, your computer must be set up on a network. To set up a computer on a network, see page 176.

SHARE A PRINTER

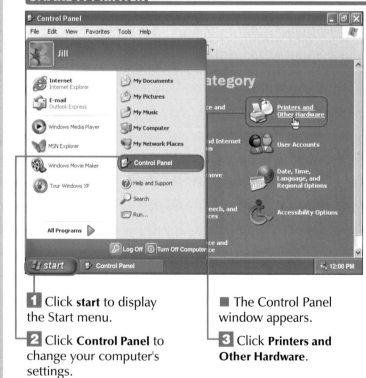

1 Click **start** to display the Start menu.

2 Click **Control Panel** to change your computer's settings.

■ The Control Panel window appears.

3 Click **Printers and Other Hardware**.

■ The Printers and Other Hardware window appears.

4 Click **View installed printers or fax printers**.

How can I tell if my printer is shared?

In the Printers and Faxes window, a hand () appears in the icon for your shared printer. Windows may have already shared your printer when you set up your computer on the network or installed the printer. You should make sure both your computer and the shared printer are turned on and are accessible when other people want to use the printer.

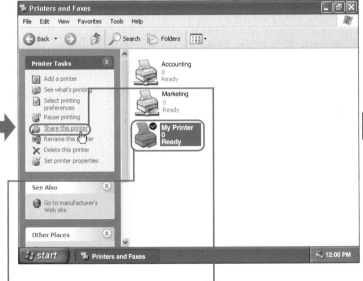

How do I stop sharing a printer?

When you no longer want people on the network to use your printer, you can stop sharing your printer. Perform steps **1** to **10** below, except select **Do not share this printer** in step **7**.

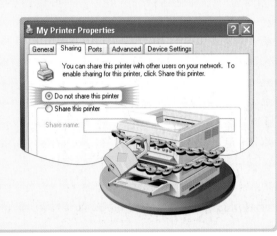

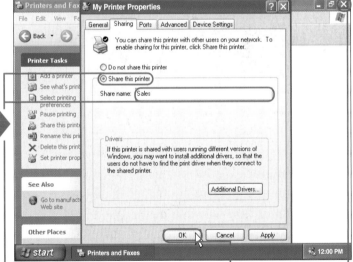

■ The Printers and Faxes window appears, displaying an icon for each printer you can use.

5 Click the printer you want to share with other people on the network.

6 Click **Share this printer**.

■ A Properties dialog box appears.

7 Click **Share this printer** to share the printer with other people on the network (○ changes to ◉).

8 This area displays the name of the printer people will see on the network. To change the printer name, type a new name.

9 Click **OK** to confirm your changes.

10 Click ✕ to close the Printers and Faxes window.

SET UP A HOME NETWORK

If you have more than one computer at home, you can set up a network so the computers can exchange information and share equipment.

Share Information

A network allows you to work with information stored on other computers on the network. Sharing information is useful when people on a network are working together on a project and need to access the same files.

Share Equipment

A network allows several computers to share equipment, such as a printer. Sharing equipment allows you to save money since several people on the network can use the same equipment.

Share an Internet Connection

You can set up a computer to share its Internet connection with other computers on the network. All the computers on the network can use the shared Internet connection to access the Internet at the same time. The computer that shares its Internet connection must be turned on when other computers on the network want to access the Internet.

Your Internet Service Provider (ISP), which is the company that gives you access to the Internet, may charge extra or not allow multiple computers to share a single Internet connection. You can contact your ISP for more information.

Protect Your Network

When you set up a network, Windows will install firewall software on the computer that shares its Internet connection. The firewall software is designed to protect your network from unauthorized access when computers on the network are connected to the Internet.

Play Multi-Player Games

Many games allow several people on a network and the Internet to compete against each other. You can obtain multi-player games at computer stores and on the Internet.

NETWORK HARDWARE

You need to install and set up your network hardware to enable the computers on your network to communicate.

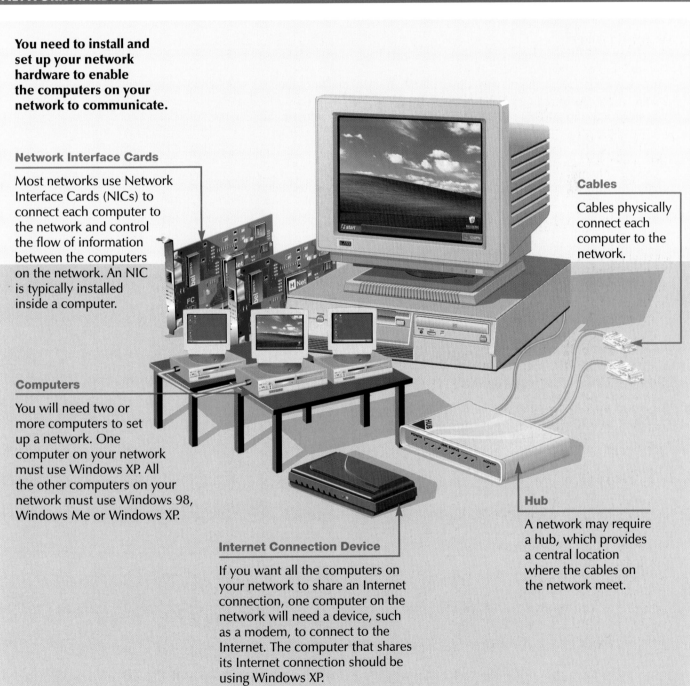

Network Interface Cards

Most networks use Network Interface Cards (NICs) to connect each computer to the network and control the flow of information between the computers on the network. An NIC is typically installed inside a computer.

Cables

Cables physically connect each computer to the network.

Computers

You will need two or more computers to set up a network. One computer on your network must use Windows XP. All the other computers on your network must use Windows 98, Windows Me or Windows XP.

Internet Connection Device

If you want all the computers on your network to share an Internet connection, one computer on the network will need a device, such as a modem, to connect to the Internet. The computer that shares its Internet connection should be using Windows XP.

Hub

A network may require a hub, which provides a central location where the cables on the network meet.

Windows provides the Network Setup Wizard that will take you step by step through the process of setting up a computer on your home network.

You must run the Network Setup Wizard on each computer you want to set up on your home network. If the computers on your network will share an Internet connection, you should run the wizard on the computer that has the Internet connection first.

SET UP A HOME NETWORK

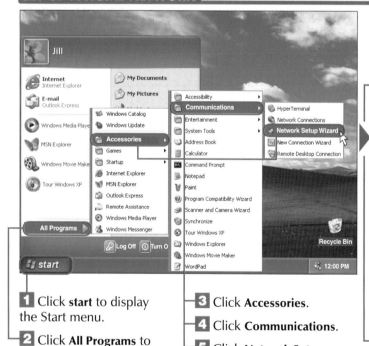

1 Click **start** to display the Start menu.

2 Click **All Programs** to view a list of the programs on your computer.

3 Click **Accessories**.

4 Click **Communications**.

5 Click **Network Setup Wizard**.

■ The Network Setup Wizard appears.

■ This area displays information about the wizard and the benefits of setting up a network.

6 Click **Next** to continue.

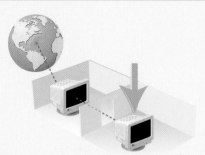

What are the most common ways a computer connects to the Internet on a home network?

You need to select the way a computer connects to the Internet in step **8** below. Here are the two most common ways a computer will connect to the Internet on a home network.

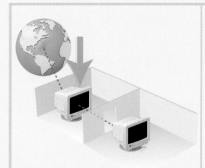

This computer connects directly to the Internet. The other computers on my network connect to the Internet through this computer.

This computer connects to the Internet through another computer on my network or through a residential gateway. A residential gateway is a hardware device that connects a network to the Internet and typically offers a high-speed connection to the Internet.

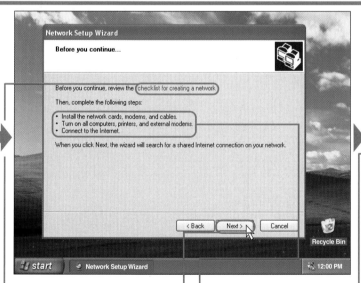

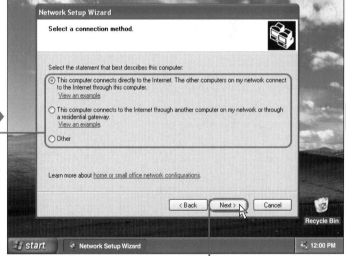

■ You can click this link to review a checklist for creating a network.

Note: If you click the link, the Help and Support Center window appears, displaying the checklist. When you finish reviewing the checklist, click ⊠ to close the window.

■ Before continuing, make sure you have completed the steps listed in this area.

7 Click **Next** to continue.

8 Click the option that best describes the way the computer connects to the Internet (○ changes to ◉).

*Note: You can click **Other** to view additional statements if the displayed statements do not describe the computer.*

9 Click **Next** to continue.

*Note: If you selected **Other** in step **8**, repeat steps **8** and **9**.*

CONTINUED

SET UP A HOME NETWORK

When setting up a computer on your network, you need to provide a description, computer name and workgroup name for the computer.

A computer name identifies the computer on your network. A workgroup name identifies the group of computers on your network that the computer belongs to.

SET UP A HOME NETWORK (CONTINUED)

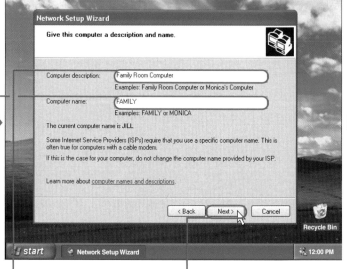

10 Click the connection the computer uses to connect to the Internet.

Note: This screen may not appear, depending on the statement you selected in step 8. If the screen does not appear, skip to step 12.

11 Click **Next** to continue.

12 Type a brief description for the computer.

13 Double-click this area and type a name for the computer.

Note: For information on selecting a computer name, see the top of page 181.

14 Click **Next** to continue.

What should I consider when choosing a computer name?

➤ Each computer on your network must have a different name.

➤ A computer name can contain up to 15 characters.

➤ A computer name cannot contain spaces or special characters, such as ; : , " < > * + = \ | or ?.

➤ Your Internet Service Provider (ISP), which is the company that gives you access to the Internet, may require you to use a specific name for the computer that shares its Internet connection. If this is true for your ISP, make sure you use the name your ISP specifies.

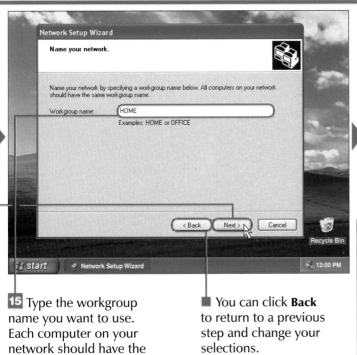

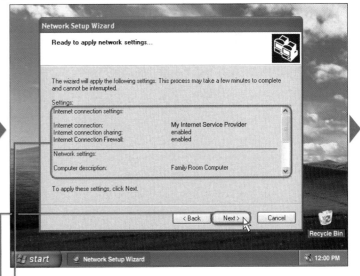

15 Type the workgroup name you want to use. Each computer on your network should have the same workgroup name.

16 Click **Next** to continue.

■ You can click **Back** to return to a previous step and change your selections.

■ This area displays the network settings that the wizard will apply to the computer.

17 Click **Next** to apply the network settings.

■ The wizard may take a few minutes to apply the network settings. This process cannot be interrupted.

CONTINUED

SET UP A HOME NETWORK

You need to specify how you want to set up other computers that use Windows 98 or Windows Me on your home network.

To set up other computers that use Windows 98 or Windows Me, you can create a Network Setup disk or use the CD you used to install Windows XP.

To set up other computers that use Windows XP, perform the steps starting on page 178 on each computer.

SET UP A HOME NETWORK (CONTINUED)

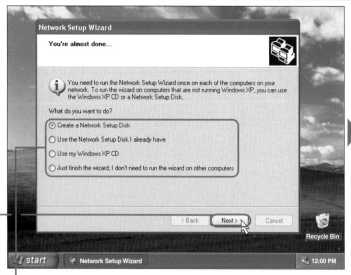

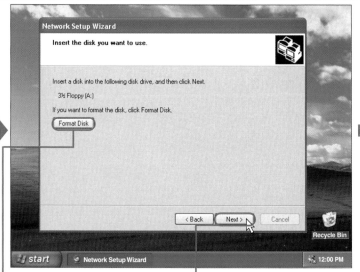

18 Click an option to specify the task you want to perform to set up other computers on your network (○ changes to ◉).

19 Click **Next** to continue.

Note: If you chose to use the Network Setup disk you already have or the Windows XP CD, skip to step 22. If you chose to just finish the wizard, skip to step 24.

20 Insert a formatted, blank floppy disk into the floppy drive.

■ If you are using an unformatted floppy disk or the disk contains files, you can click **Format Disk** to format the disk.

Note: Formatting a disk will permanently remove all the information on the disk.

21 Click **Next** to continue.

What resources can I share on my network?

After you set up your network, you can share folders and your printer with other computers on the network. The Network Setup Wizard automatically shares your Shared Documents folder and your printer. For information on the Shared Documents folder, see page 126. For information on sharing folders and printers, see pages 172 and 174.

How can I view all the folders that are shared on my network?

You can use **My Network Places** to access all the folders that are shared by your computer and other computers on your network. To use My Network Places, see page 170.

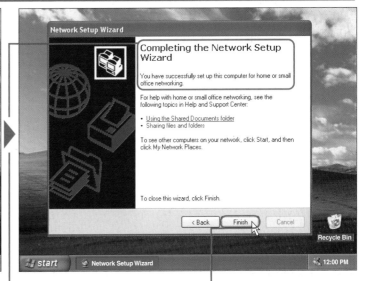

■ The wizard displays the steps you need to perform to set up other computers on your network. The displayed steps depend on the option you selected in step **18**.

22 Click **Next** to continue.

■ This message appears when you have successfully set up the computer on your network.

23 If you created a Network Setup disk, remove the floppy disk from the drive.

24 Click **Finish** to close the wizard.

■ A message may appear, stating that you must restart the computer before the new settings will take effect. Click **Yes** to restart the computer.

CHAPTER 9

BROWSE THE WEB

This chapter will explain how the World Wide Web works and how you can use it to transfer information to your computer from Web sites around the world.

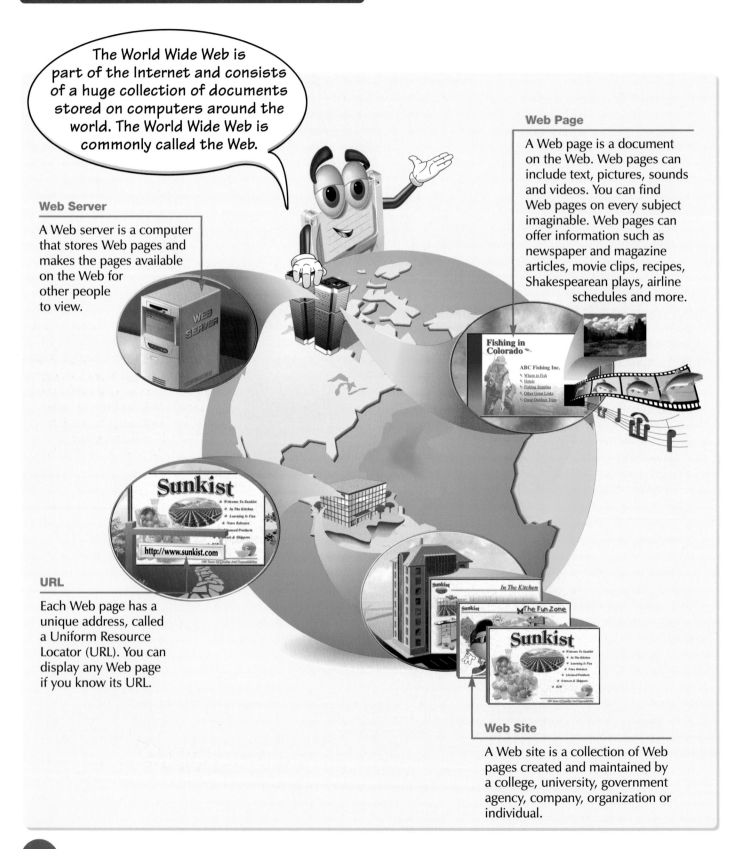

The World Wide Web is part of the Internet and consists of a huge collection of documents stored on computers around the world. The World Wide Web is commonly called the Web.

Web Page

A Web page is a document on the Web. Web pages can include text, pictures, sounds and videos. You can find Web pages on every subject imaginable. Web pages can offer information such as newspaper and magazine articles, movie clips, recipes, Shakespearean plays, airline schedules and more.

Web Server

A Web server is a computer that stores Web pages and makes the pages available on the Web for other people to view.

URL

Each Web page has a unique address, called a Uniform Resource Locator (URL). You can display any Web page if you know its URL.

Web Site

A Web site is a collection of Web pages created and maintained by a college, university, government agency, company, organization or individual.

Web Browser

A Web browser is a program that allows you to view and explore information on the Web. Windows XP comes with the Microsoft Internet Explorer Web browser.

Links

Web pages contain links, which are highlighted text or images on a Web page that connect to other pages on the Web. You can select a link to display a Web page located on the same computer or on a computer across the city, country or world. Links are also known as hyperlinks.

Links allow you to easily navigate through a vast amount of information by jumping from one Web page to another. This is known as "browsing the Web."

Connecting to the Internet

Most people connect to the Internet using a company called an Internet Service Provider (ISP). Once you pay your ISP to connect to the Internet, you can view and exchange information on the Internet free of charge.

Most individuals use a modem to connect to the Internet, although cable modems and Digital Subscriber Line (DSL) modems are becoming more popular. Most schools and businesses connect to the Internet through a network connection.

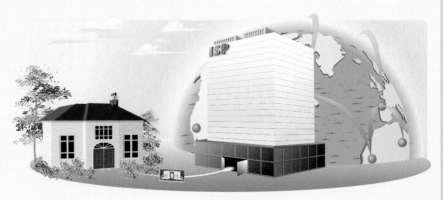

You can start Internet Explorer to browse through the information on the Web.

The first time you start Internet Explorer, the New Connection Wizard will appear if you have not yet set up your connection to the Internet. Follow the instructions in the wizard to set up your Internet connection.

START INTERNET EXPLORER

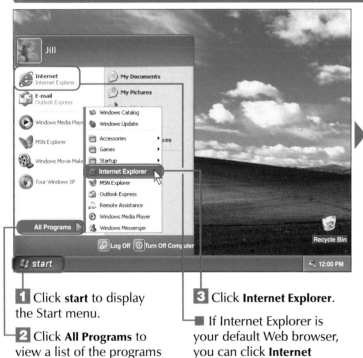

1 Click **start** to display the Start menu.

2 Click **All Programs** to view a list of the programs on your computer.

3 Click **Internet Explorer**.

■ If Internet Explorer is your default Web browser, you can click **Internet** instead of performing steps **2** and **3**.

■ The Microsoft Internet Explorer window appears, displaying your home page.

Note: If you are not currently connected to the Internet, a dialog box will appear that allows you to connect.

4 When you finish browsing through the information on the Web, click **X** to close the Microsoft Internet Explorer window.

A link connects text or an image on one Web page to another Web page. When you select the text or image, the linked Web page appears.

Links allow you to easily navigate through a vast amount of information by jumping from one Web page to another. Links are also known as hyperlinks.

SELECT A LINK

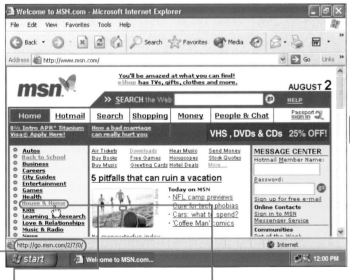

1 Position the mouse ⤵ over a highlighted word or image of interest. The mouse ⤵ changes to a hand ⬆ when over a link.

■ This area displays the address of the Web page that the link will take you to.

2 Click the word or image to display the linked Web page.

■ The linked Web page appears.

■ This area shows the progress of the transfer.

■ This area displays the title of the Web page.

■ This area displays the address of the Web page.

DISPLAY A SPECIFIC WEB PAGE

You can display any page on the Web that you have heard or read about.

Check out www.sunkist.com

You need to know the address of the Web page that you want to view. Each page on the Web has a unique address, called a Uniform Resource Locator (URL).

DISPLAY A SPECIFIC WEB PAGE

1 Click this area to highlight the current Web page address.

2 Type the address of the Web page you want to display and then press the **Enter** key.

*Note: You do not need to type **http://** when typing a Web page address. For example, you do not need to type **http://** in front of www.walmart.com.*

■ This area shows the progress of the transfer.

■ The Web page appears on your screen.

What are some popular Web pages that I can display?

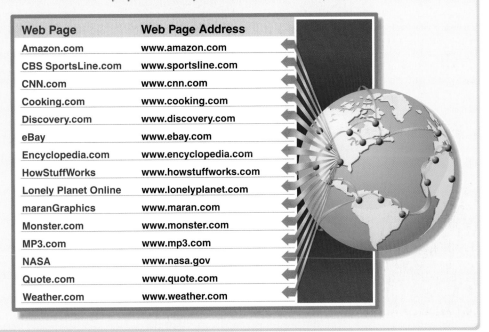

Web Page	Web Page Address
Amazon.com	www.amazon.com
CBS SportsLine.com	www.sportsline.com
CNN.com	www.cnn.com
Cooking.com	www.cooking.com
Discovery.com	www.discovery.com
eBay	www.ebay.com
Encyclopedia.com	www.encyclopedia.com
HowStuffWorks	www.howstuffworks.com
Lonely Planet Online	www.lonelyplanet.com
maranGraphics	www.maran.com
Monster.com	www.monster.com
MP3.com	www.mp3.com
NASA	www.nasa.gov
Quote.com	www.quote.com
Weather.com	www.weather.com

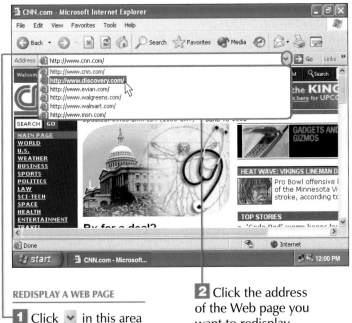

REDISPLAY A WEB PAGE

1 Click ⌄ in this area to display the addresses of the Web pages you have recently displayed.

2 Click the address of the Web page you want to redisplay.

■ The Web page you selected appears on your screen.

QUICKLY REDISPLAY A WEB PAGE

1 If you begin typing the address of a Web page you have recently displayed, a list of matching addresses automatically appears.

2 Click the address of the Web page you want to redisplay.

191

If a Web page is taking a long time to appear on your screen, you can stop the transfer of the page.

You may also want to stop the transfer of a Web page if you realize a page contains information that does not interest you.

STOP TRANSFER OF A WEB PAGE

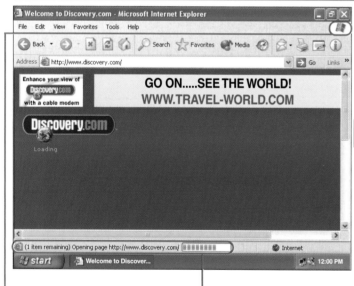

■ This icon is animated as a Web page transfers to your computer.

■ This area shows the progress of the transfer.

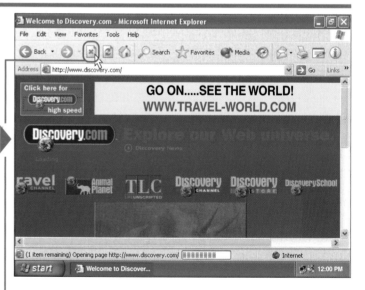

1 Click ⬛ to stop the transfer of the Web page.

■ If you stopped the transfer of the Web page because the page was taking too long to appear, you may want to try displaying the page at a later time.

You can easily move back and forth through the Web pages you have viewed since you last started Internet Explorer.

MOVE THROUGH WEB PAGES

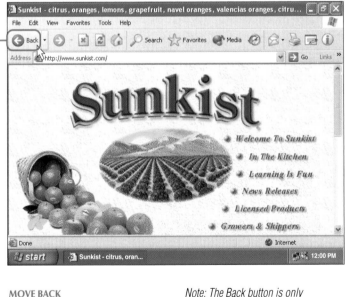

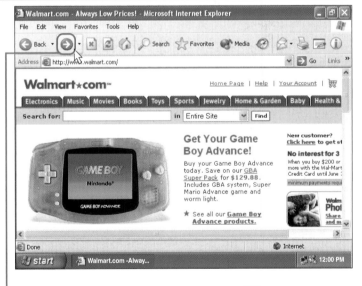

MOVE BACK

1 Click **Back** to return to the last Web page you viewed.

Note: The Back button is only available if you have viewed more than one Web page since you last started Internet Explorer.

MOVE FORWARD

1 Click to move forward through the Web pages you have viewed.

Note: The button is only available after you use the Back button to return to a Web page.

You can display and change the Web page that appears each time you start Internet Explorer. This page is called your home page.

DISPLAY AND CHANGE YOUR HOME PAGE

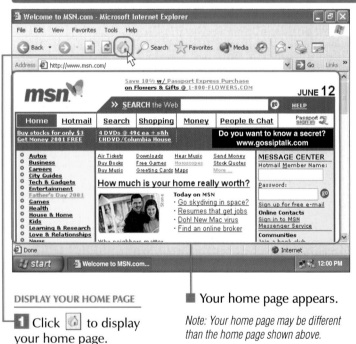

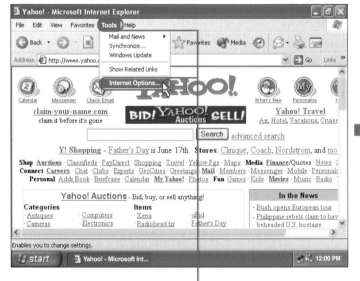

DISPLAY YOUR HOME PAGE

1 Click 🏠 to display your home page.

■ Your home page appears.

Note: Your home page may be different than the home page shown above.

CHANGE YOUR HOME PAGE

1 Display the Web page you want to set as your home page.

Note: To display a specific Web page, see page 190.

2 Click **Tools**.

3 Click **Internet Options**.

SIMPLIFY IT

Which Web page should I set as my home page?

You can set any page on the Web as your home page. The page you choose should be a page you want to frequently visit. You may want to choose a page that provides a good starting point for exploring the Web, such as www.yahoo.com, or a page that provides information about your personal interests or work.

SIMPLIFY IT

How can I once again use my original home page?

To once again use your original home page, perform steps **1** to **5** starting on page 194, except select **Use Default** in step **4**. In most cases, the www.msn.com Web page is the original home page.

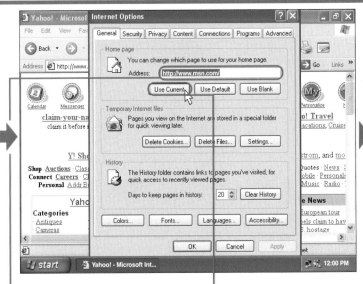

■ The Internet Options dialog box appears.

■ This area displays the address of your current home page.

4 Click **Use Current** to set the Web page displayed on your screen as your new home page.

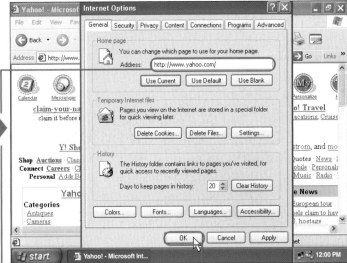

■ This area displays the address of your new home page.

5 Click **OK** to confirm your change.

You can search for Web pages that discuss topics of interest to you.

Internet Explorer uses the MSN search tool to help you find Web pages. A search tool is a service on the Web that catalogs Web pages to help you find pages of interest.

SEARCH THE WEB

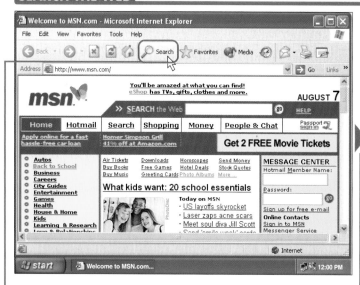

1 Click **Search** to search for Web pages of interest.

■ The Search Companion area appears.

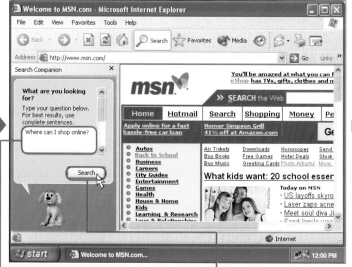

2 Click this area and then type a question that describes the information you want to search for.

3 Click **Search** to start the search.

Is there another way to search for information on the Web?

Yes. Many Web sites allow you to search for information on the Web. These Web sites can also allow you to browse through categories, such as

news, sports and weather, to find Web pages of interest. Here are some popular Web sites that allow you to search for information on the Web.

Google

www.google.com

Lycos

www.lycos.com

Yahoo!

www.yahoo.com

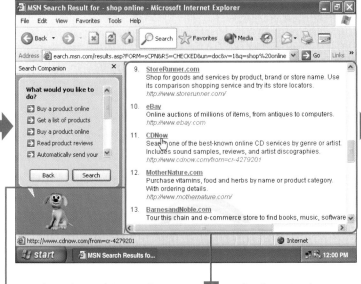

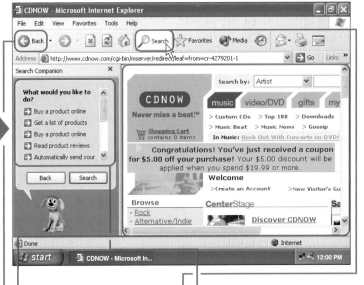

■ A list of matching Web pages and their descriptions appear in this area.

4 To display a Web page, click the Web page of interest.

■ The Web page you selected appears in this area.

■ You can click **Back** to return to the list of Web pages and select another Web page.

■ This area may display a list of options you can select to narrow your search. The Search Companion will ask you questions to help you find Web pages of interest.

5 When you finish searching, click **Search** to hide the Search Companion area.

You can use the Favorites feature to create a list of Web pages that you frequently visit. The Favorites feature allows you to quickly display a favorite Web page at any time.

Selecting Web pages from your list of favorites saves you from having to remember and constantly retype the same Web page addresses over and over again.

ADD A WEB PAGE TO FAVORITES

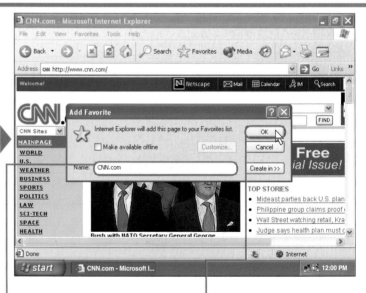

1 Display the Web page you want to add to your list of favorite Web pages.

Note: To display a specific Web page, see page 190.

2 Click **Favorites**.

3 Click **Add to Favorites**.

■ The Add Favorite dialog box appears.

■ The name of the Web page appears in this area.

4 Click **OK** to add the Web page to your list of favorites.

Does Internet Explorer automatically add Web pages to my list of favorites?

Yes. Internet Explorer automatically adds the Links folder and the following Web pages to your list of favorites.

Links folder

Contains several useful Web pages, such as the Free Hotmail page, which allows you to set up and use a free e-mail account.

MSN.com

A Web site provided by Microsoft that offers a great starting point for exploring the Web.

Radio Station Guide

Allows you to listen to radio stations from around the world that broadcast on the Internet.

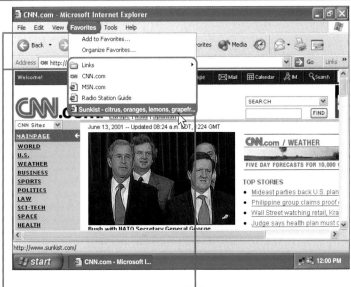

VIEW A FAVORITE WEB PAGE

1 Click **Favorites**.

■ A list of your favorite Web pages appears.

Note: If the entire list does not appear, position the mouse over the bottom of the menu to browse through the entire list.

2 Click the favorite Web page you want to view.

Note: To display the favorite Web pages in a folder, click the folder (📁) before performing step 2.

■ The favorite Web page you selected appears.

■ You can repeat steps **1** and **2** to view another favorite Web page.

CHAPTER 10

EXCHANGE E-MAIL

You can exchange e-mail messages with friends, family members and colleagues from around the world. In this chapter, you will learn how to read, send and work with messages.

You can start Outlook Express to open and read the contents of your e-mail messages.

Chris,

The drafts for the advertising campaign are ready. Will you be free at 2:00 p.m. tomorrow to discuss them?

Henry

The first time you start Outlook Express, a wizard will appear if you have not yet set up your Internet connection or e-mail account. Follow the instructions in the wizard to set up your Internet connection and/or e-mail account.

READ MESSAGES

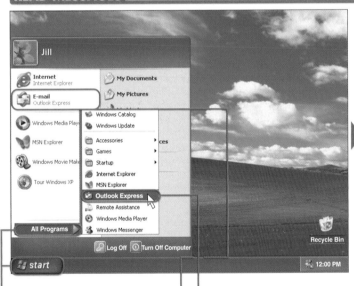

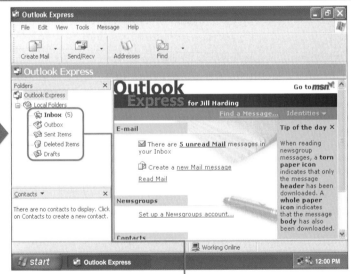

START OUTLOOK EXPRESS

1 Click **start** to display the Start menu.

2 Click **All Programs** to view a list of the programs on your computer.

3 Click **Outlook Express**.

■ If Outlook Express is your default e-mail program, you can click **E-mail** instead of performing steps **2** and **3**.

■ The Outlook Express window appears.

Note: If you are not currently connected to the Internet, a dialog box will appear that allows you to connect.

READ MESSAGES

■ This area displays the folders that contain your messages.

Note: A number in brackets beside a folder indicates how many unread messages the folder contains. The number disappears when you have read all the messages in the folder.

202

What folders does Outlook Express use
to store my messages?

Inbox

Stores messages
sent to you.

Outbox

Temporarily stores
messages that
have not yet been
sent.

Sent Items

Stores copies of
messages you
have sent.

Deleted Items

Stores messages
you have deleted.

Drafts

Stores messages
you have not yet
completed.

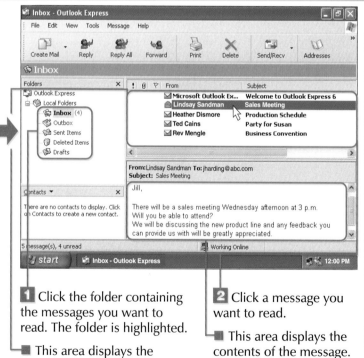

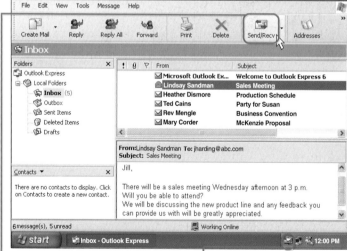

1 Click the folder containing
the messages you want to
read. The folder is highlighted.

■ This area displays the
messages in the folder you
selected. Unread messages
display a closed envelope (✉)
and appear in **bold** type.

2 Click a message you
want to read.

■ This area displays the
contents of the message.

CHECK FOR NEW MESSAGES

**When you are connected
to the Internet, Outlook
Express automatically
checks for new messages
every 30 minutes.**

1 To immediately check
for new messages, click
Send/Recv.

■ When you have new
messages, a new e-mail
icon (✉) appears in
this area.

You can send a message to express an idea or request information.

To practice sending a message, you can send a message to yourself.

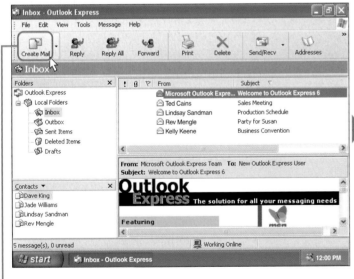

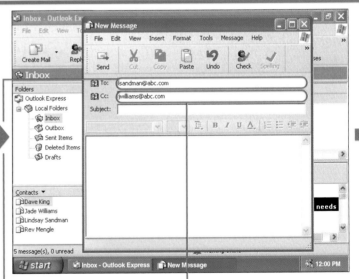

1 Click **Create Mail** to send a new message.

■ The New Message window appears.

2 Type the e-mail address of the person you want to receive the message.

3 To send a copy of the message to a person who is not directly involved but would be interested in the message, click this area and then type the person's e-mail address.

Note: To send the message to more than one person, separate each e-mail address with a semicolon (;).

How can I express emotions in my e-mail messages?

You can use special characters, called smileys, to express emotions in e-mail messages. These characters resemble human faces if you turn them sideways.

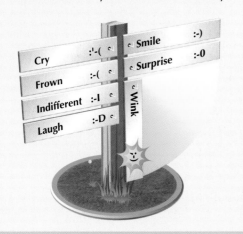

Cry	:'-(
Frown	:-(
Indifferent	:-I
Laugh	:-D
Smile	:-)
Surprise	:-0
Wink	;-)

What should I consider when sending a message?

A MESSAGE WRITTEN IN CAPITAL LETTERS IS ANNOYING AND DIFFICULT TO READ. THIS IS CALLED SHOUTING. Always use upper and lower case letters when typing e-mail messages.

HOW ARE YOU?

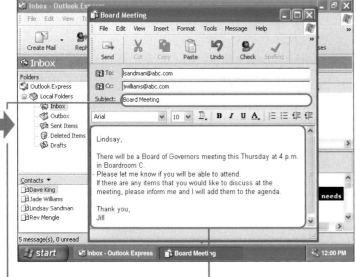

4 Click this area and then type the subject of the message.

5 Click this area and then type the message.

6 Click **Send** to send the message.

■ Outlook Express sends the message and stores a copy of the message in the Sent Items folder.

REPLY TO A MESSAGE

You can reply to a message to answer a question, express an opinion or supply additional information.

Yes, and I will bring the report to our lunch meeting tomorrow.

Tamara

REPLY TO A MESSAGE

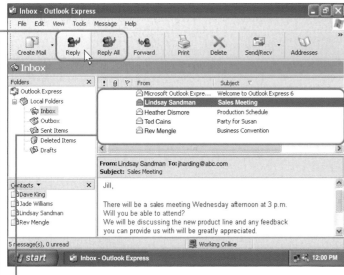

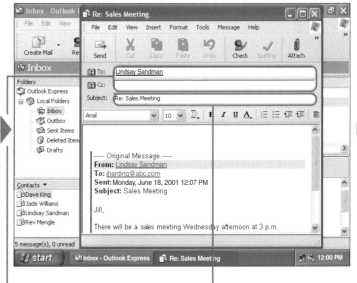

1 Click the message you want to reply to.

2 Click the reply option you want to use.

Reply
Sends a reply to only the author.

Reply All
Sends a reply to the author and everyone who received the original message.

■ A window appears for you to compose your reply.

■ Outlook Express fills in the e-mail address(es) for you.

■ Outlook Express also fills in the subject, starting the subject with **Re:**.

How can I save time
when typing a message?

You can use abbreviations
for words and phrases
to save time when typing
messages. Here are
some commonly used
abbreviations.

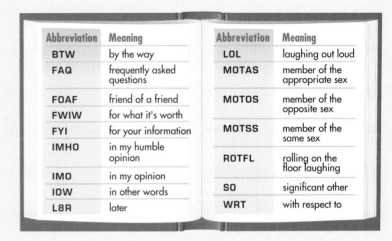

Abbreviation	Meaning
BTW	by the way
FAQ	frequently asked questions
FOAF	friend of a friend
FWIW	for what it's worth
FYI	for your information
IMHO	in my humble opinion
IMO	in my opinion
IOW	in other words
L8R	later

Abbreviation	Meaning
LOL	laughing out loud
MOTAS	member of the appropriate sex
MOTOS	member of the opposite sex
MOTSS	member of the same sex
ROTFL	rolling on the floor laughing
SO	significant other
WRT	with respect to

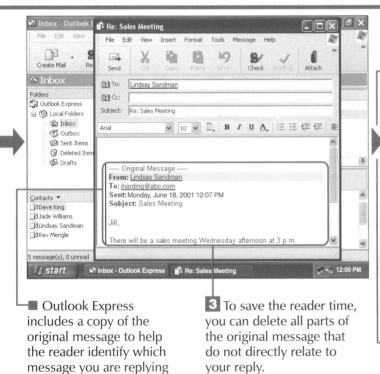

■ Outlook Express
includes a copy of the
original message to help
the reader identify which
message you are replying
to. This is called quoting.

3 To save the reader time,
you can delete all parts of
the original message that
do not directly relate to
your reply.

4 Click this area and
then type your reply.

5 Click **Send** to send
the reply.

■ Outlook Express stores
a copy of the message in
the Sent Items folder.

FORWARD A MESSAGE

After reading a message, you can add comments and then forward the message to a friend, family member or colleague.

Forwarding a message is useful when you know another person would be interested in the message.

FORWARD A MESSAGE

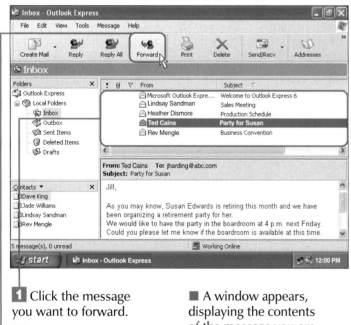

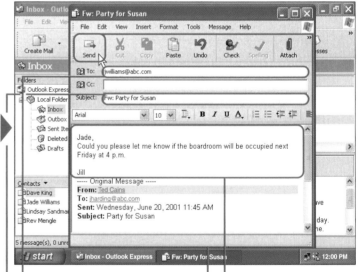

1 Click the message you want to forward.

2 Click **Forward**.

■ A window appears, displaying the contents of the message you are forwarding.

3 Type the e-mail address of the person you want to receive the message.

■ Outlook Express fills in the subject for you, starting the subject with **Fw:**.

4 Click this area and then type any comments about the message you are forwarding.

5 Click **Send** to forward the message.

PRINT A MESSAGE

You can produce a paper copy of a message.

Outlook Express prints the page number and total number of pages at the top of each page. The current date prints at the bottom of each page.

PRINT A MESSAGE

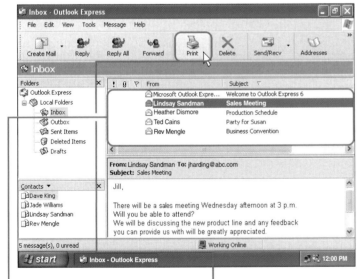

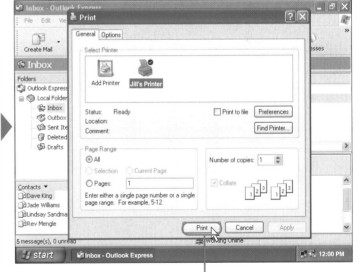

1 Click the message you want to print.

2 Click **Print** to print the message.

■ The Print dialog box appears.

3 Click **Print** to print the entire message.

ATTACH A FILE TO A MESSAGE

You can attach a file to a message you are sending. Attaching a file to a message is useful when you want to include additional information with a message.

From:
To:
Subject:
Cc:

This year's charity golf was a huge success! I would like to thank all the volunteers for organizing a fantastic event. This year's winner was Mike Wilson. I have attached a photo of one of his winning drives!

ATTACH A FILE TO A MESSAGE

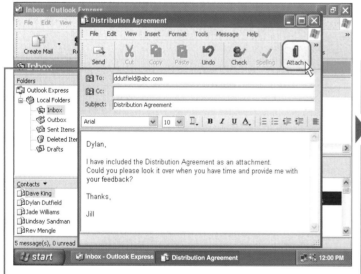

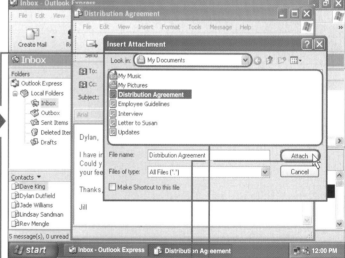

1 To create a message, perform steps **1** to **5** starting on page 204.

2 Click **Attach** to attach a file to the message.

Note: If the Attach button does not appear in the window, you need to enlarge the window to display the button. To resize a window, see page 9.

■ The Insert Attachment dialog box appears.

■ This area shows the location of the displayed files. You can click this area to change the location.

3 Click the name of the file you want to attach to the message.

4 Click **Attach** to attach the file to the message.

What types of files can I attach to a message?

You can attach many types of files to a message, including documents, pictures, videos, sounds and programs. The computer receiving the message must have the necessary hardware and software installed to display or play the file you attach.

Can I attach a large file to a message?

The company that provides your e-mail account will usually limit the size of the messages that you can send and receive over the Internet. Most companies do not allow you to send or receive messages larger than 2 MB, which includes all attached files.

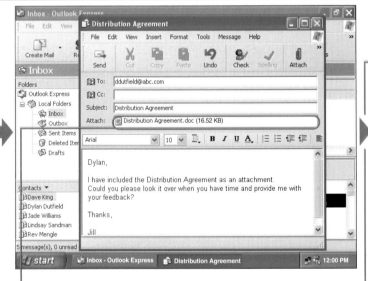

■ This area displays the name and size of the file you selected.

■ To attach additional files to the message, perform steps **2** to **4** for each file you want to attach.

5 Click **Send** to send the message.

■ Outlook Express will send the message and the attached file(s) to the e-mail address(es) you specified.

OPEN AN ATTACHED FILE

> You can easily open a file attached to a message you receive.

jnelson@xyzcorp.com

Before opening an attached file, make sure the file is from a reliable source. Some files can contain viruses, which can damage the information on your computer. You can use an anti-virus program, such as McAfee VirusScan, to check files for viruses.

OPEN AN ATTACHED FILE

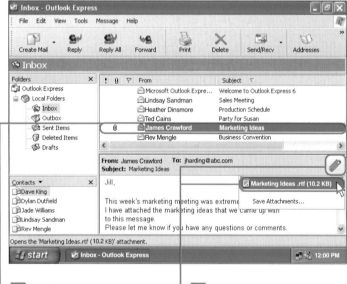

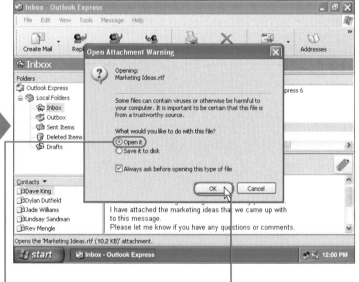

1 Click a message with an attached file. A message with an attached file displays a paper clip icon (🔋).

2 Click the paper clip icon (🖉) in this area to display a list of the files attached to the message.

3 Click the name of the file you want to open.

■ A dialog box may appear, asking if you want to open or save the file.

4 Click **Open it** to open the file (○ changes to ◉).

5 Click **OK** to open the file.

DELETE A MESSAGE

You can delete a message you no longer need. Deleting messages prevents your folders from becoming cluttered with messages.

DELETE A MESSAGE

1 Click the message you want to delete.

2 Click **Delete** to delete the message.

■ Outlook Express removes the message from the current folder and places the message in the Deleted Items folder.

Note: Deleting a message from the Deleted Items folder will permanently remove the message from your computer.

CHAPTER 11

EXCHANGE INSTANT MESSAGES

Read this chapter to find out how to exchange instant messages with your friends using Windows Messenger.

You can use Windows Messenger to see when your friends are online and exchange instant messages and files with them.

START WINDOWS MESSENGER

1 Click **start** to display the Start menu.

2 Click **All Programs** to view a list of the programs on your computer.

3 Click **Windows Messenger**.

■ You can also double-click this icon (🖾) to start Windows Messenger.

Note: If 🖾 is hidden, you can click ◀ on the taskbar to display the icon.

■ The Windows Messenger window appears.

■ If you are already signed in to Windows Messenger, you do not need to perform steps 4 to 6.

4 Click this link to sign in to Windows Messenger.

Note: If you are not currently connected to the Internet, a dialog box appears, allowing you to connect.

Why does a wizard appear when I start Windows Messenger?

The first time you start Windows Messenger, a wizard appears to help you add a Passport to your user account. You must add a Passport to your user account to use Windows Messenger. Follow the instructions in the wizard to add a Passport to your user account.

How can I sign out of Windows Messenger?

When you finish using Windows Messenger, you can sign out of the service.

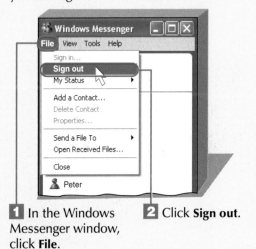

1 In the Windows Messenger window, click **File**.

2 Click **Sign out**.

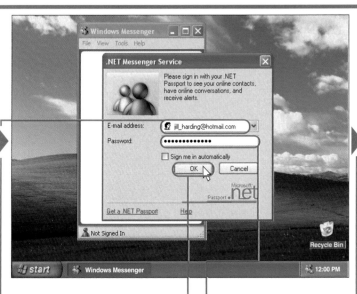

■ The .NET Messenger Service dialog box appears.

■ This area displays your e-mail address.

5 Type your password. Make sure you type the uppercase and lowercase letters exactly.

6 Click **OK** to sign in.

■ If you have added contacts to your list, this area displays the contacts that are currently online and not online.

Note: To add contacts to your list, see page 218.

■ You can click this link to read your e-mail messages. If you have a Hotmail e-mail account, the link displays the number of new e-mail messages you have received.

217

You can add a person to your contact list to see when they are online and available to exchange instant messages.

Windows Messenger allows you to add up to 150 people to your contact list.

ADD A CONTACT

■ This area displays each person you have added to your contact list. You can see the contacts that are currently online and not online.

1 Click **Add** to add a person to your contact list.

■ The Add a Contact wizard appears.

2 Click this option to add a contact by specifying the person's e-mail address (○ changes to ◉).

3 Click **Next** to continue.

Who can I add to my contact list?

Each person you want to add to your contact list requires a Passport. A Passport is obtained when Windows Messenger is set up on a computer. People using a program that is compatible with Windows Messenger can obtain a Passport at the passport.com Web site.

How do I remove a person from my contact list?

In the Windows Messenger window, click the name of the person you want to remove from your contact list and then press the Delete key. The person will no longer appear in your contact list.

-4 Type the person's e-mail address.

5 Click **Next** to continue.

■ This message appears if the wizard added the person to your contact list.

6 Click **Finish** to close the wizard.

■ The person appears in your contact list.

Note: Windows Messenger will notify the person that you added them to your contact list.

SEND AN INSTANT MESSAGE

You can send an instant message to a person in your contact list. The person must be currently signed in to Windows Messenger.

Bill: How is the weather over there?

For information on adding a person to your contact list, see page 218.

When sending instant messages, never give out your password or credit card information.

SEND AN INSTANT MESSAGE

1 Double-click the name of the person you want to send an instant message to.

■ The Conversation window appears.

2 Click this area and type your message.

Note: A message can be up to 400 characters long.

3 Click **Send** to send the message.

Note: You can also press the **Enter** *key to send the message.*

220

How can I express emotions in my instant messages?

If you type one of the following sets of characters, Windows Messenger will automatically replace the characters with an image, called an emoticon. Emoticons allow you to express emotions in your instant messages.

Type	Windows Messenger Sends	Type	Windows Messenger Sends
:p	☺	(d)	🍸
(y)	👍	(i)	💡
(g)	🎁	(S)	🌙ᶻ
(f)	🌹	(*)	⭐

What should I consider when sending an instant message?

A MESSAGE WRITTEN IN CAPITAL LETTERS IS ANNOYING AND DIFFICULT TO READ. THIS IS CALLED SHOUTING. Always use upper and lower case letters when typing an instant message.

■ This area displays the message you sent and the ongoing conversation.

■ This area displays the date and time the other person last sent you a message. If the other person is typing a message, this area indicates that the person is typing.

4 When you finish exchanging messages, click ✕ to close the Conversation window.

RECEIVE AN INSTANT MESSAGE

■ When you receive an instant message that is not part of an ongoing conversation, your computer makes a sound and briefly displays a box containing the first part of the message.

1 To display the entire message, click inside the box.

Note: You can also click the Conversation button on the taskbar to display the entire message.

■ The Conversation window appears, displaying the message.

SEND A FILE

While exchanging instant messages with another person, you can send the person a file.

If your computer is connected to a network with a firewall, you may not be able to send a file.

SEND A FILE

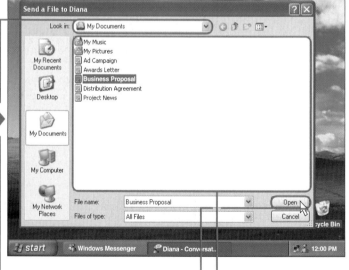

1 While exchanging instant messages with another person, click **Send a file**.

Note: For information on sending instant messages, see page 220.

■ The Send a File dialog box appears.

■ This area shows the location of the displayed files. You can click this area to change the location.

2 Click the file you want to send.

3 Click **Open** to send the file.

What types of files can I send?

You can send many types of files, including documents, pictures, sounds, videos and programs. The computer receiving the file must have the necessary hardware and software installed to display or play the file.

Is there another way that I can send a file?

You can also send a file by attaching the file to an e-mail message. This is useful when you want to send a file to a person who is not currently signed in to Windows Messenger. To attach a file to an e-mail message, see page 210.

■ This area displays the status of the file transfer. The other person must accept the file before the file will transfer.

■ If you no longer want to send the file, you can click **Cancel** to stop the transfer of the file.

*Note: After the other person accepts the file, the **Cancel** option is no longer available.*

■ This message appears when the other person accepts the file.

■ This message appears when the file transfer is complete.

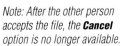

223

INDEX

TRADE & INDIVIDUAL ORDERS

Phone: **(800) 762-2974**
or **(317) 572-3993**
(8 a.m.–6 p.m., CST, weekdays)
FAX : **(800) 550-2747**
or **(317) 572-4002**

EDUCATIONAL ORDERS & DISCOUNTS

Phone: **(800) 434-2086**
(8:30 a.m.–5:00 p.m., CST, weekdays)
FAX : **(317) 572-4005**

CORPORATE ORDERS FOR VISUAL™ SERIES

Phone: **(800) 469-6616**
(8 a.m.–5 p.m., EST, weekdays)
FAX : **(905) 890-9434**

Qty	ISBN	Title	Price	Total

Shipping & Handling Charges

	Description	First book	Each add'l. book	Total
Domestic	Normal	$4.50	$1.50	$
	Two Day Air	$8.50	$2.50	$
	Overnight	$18.00	$3.00	$
International	Surface	$8.00	$8.00	$
	Airmail	$16.00	$16.00	$
	DHL Air	$17.00	$17.00	$

Subtotal _____

CA residents add
applicable sales tax _____

IN, MA and MD
residents add
5% sales tax _____

IL residents add
6.25% sales tax _____

RI residents add
7% sales tax _____

TX residents add
8.25% sales tax _____

Shipping _____

Total _____

Ship to:

Name _____

Address _____

Company _____

City/State/Zip _____

Daytime Phone _____

Payment: ☐ Check to Hungry Minds (US Funds Only)
               ☐ Visa   ☐ Mastercard   ☐ American Express

Card # _____ Exp. _____ Signature _____

Hungry Minds™

maranGraphics®